515

Functions

The School Mathematics Project

CAMBRIDGE
UNIVERSITY PRESS

Main authors	Simon Baxter
	Stan Dolan
	Doug French
	Andy Hall
	Barrie Hunt
	Lorna Lyons
	Paul Roder
Team leader	Barrie Hunt
Project director	Stan Dolan

0003128 9

The authors would like to give special thanks to Ann White for her help in producing the trial edition and in preparing this book for publication.

PUBLISHED BY THE PRESS SYNDICATE OF THE UNIVERSITY OF CAMBRIDGE
The Pitt Building, Trumpington Street, Cambridge CB2 1RP, United Kingdom

CAMBRIDGE UNIVERSITY PRESS
The Edinburgh Building, Cambridge CB2 2RU, United Kingdom
40 West 20th Street, New York, NY 10011–4211, USA
10 Stamford Road, Oakleigh, Melbourne 3166, Australia

First published 1991
Third printing 1996

Produced by Gecko Limited, Bicester, Oxon.

Cover design by Iguana Creative Design

Printed in the United Kingdom at the University Press, Cambridge

British Library cataloguing in publication data

A catalogue record for this book is available from the British Library

ISBN 0 521 38847 3

Contents

1 Algebra of functions

1.1 Composition of functions

Temperatures are often measured in degrees Celsius or degrees Fahrenheit. On the Fahrenheit scale, water freezes at 32°F and boils at 212°F. The Celsius scale is such that water freezes at 0°C and boils at 100°C.

> Show that the function f given by
>
> $$f(t) = \tfrac{5}{9}(t - 32)$$
>
> converts a temperature of t degrees Fahrenheit to Celsius.

Temperature is a measure of the vibration of molecules and at −273°C molecules are no longer vibrating, so −273°C is the lowest temperature that can be obtained. This temperature is called 0 on the Kelvin scale, or 0 K.

In order to convert from Celsius to Kelvin the function g is used:

$$g(t) = t + 273$$

(a) What is (i) 122°F in °C, (ii) 300°C in K, (iii) 122°F in K?

(b) What is the general rule for converting °F into K?

The rule for converting from °F directly into K can be illustrated by using an arrow graph or a flow diagram.

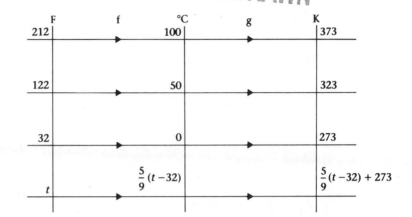

The resulting function is the **composition** of the two functions f and g.

Note that, since f(122) = 50, you can write g(50) as g (f(122)) or, with fewer brackets, as gf(122). So, contrary to what might be expected, the notation for f followed by g is gf.

What does fg(*t*) mean?

TASKSHEET 1S — Functions of functions (page 22)

E X A M P L E 1

If f and g are the functions given by f(*x*) = x^2 and g(*x*) = 2*x* + 3, then find the functions fg and gf.

S O L U T I O N

fg(*x*) = f(g(*x*)) = f(2*x* + 3) = (2*x* + 3)²

gf(*x*) = g(f(*x*)) = g(x^2) = 2x^2 + 3

5

EXERCISE 1

1 For each of the functions f and g defined below, evaluate,
(i) fg(x), (ii) gf(x).

(a) $f(x) = 2x + 3$, $g(x) = x^3$

(b) $f(x) = 2x + 1$, $g(x) = \dfrac{1}{x}$

(c) $f(x) = 3x + 2$, $g(x) = 5 - x$

(d) $f(x) = 1 - x^2$, $g(x) = 1 - 2x$

2 On a gas bill the cost of x therms of gas used by a consumer is given by £c, where

$$c(x) = 9 + 0.4x$$

A gas meter indicates the amount of gas in cubic feet used by a consumer. The number of therms of heat from x cubic feet of gas is given by the function t:

$$t(x) = 1.034x$$

(a) Find the function ct.

(b) What does ct(x) represent?

3 Each of the following is of the form fg(x). Identify f(x) and g(x).

(a) $\dfrac{1}{2x + 3}$ (b) $2\sqrt{x} - 1$ (c) $\dfrac{1}{x^2} + 3$

(d) $(2x + 1)^4$ (e) $x^8 - 4x^4 - 3$

 TASKSHEET 2E – Functions of functions (page 23)

1.2 **Range and domain**

You have seen that the function $f(t) = \frac{5}{9}(t - 32)$ converts °F to °C.

The lowest attainable temperature is $-273\,°C$ and this places a corresponding restriction on temperatures in °F.

> The set of values for which a function is defined is called the **domain** and the set of values which the function can take is called the **range**.

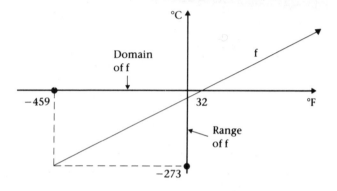

In a Cartesian graph of a function, the **domain** is all or part of the **x-axis** and the **range** is all or part of the **y-axis**.

For example, the function

$$f(x) = x^2 - 2x$$

has domain all real numbers but the range consists only of the real numbers greater than or equal to -1, that is $\{y \in \mathbb{R} : y \geq -1\}$.

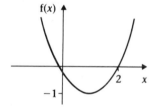

The function

$$f(x) = \sqrt{(x + 4)}$$

has domain $\{x \in \mathbb{R} : x \geq -4\}$ and range $\{y \in \mathbb{R} : y \geq 0\}$.

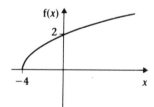

When only the formula for a function is given, it is natural to take as the domain **all** the numbers for which the formula can be worked out; for example, given the function g such that

$$g(x) = \frac{1}{x - 1}$$

you would assume that the domain is all numbers except 1. The range is then all numbers except 0, as can be seen from the graph.

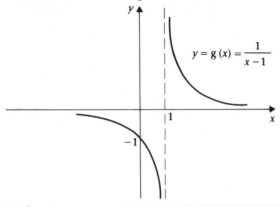

Give the natural domain and find the corresponding range for the function h such that

$$h(x) = \frac{1}{x^2}$$

Two values in the domain of a function can correspond to the same value in the range. Such a function is said to be **many-to-one**.

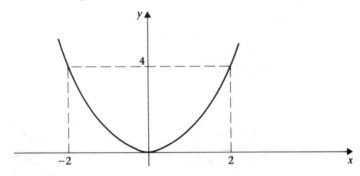

Give an example of a function which is one-to-one.

However, it is a convention that a value in a function's domain **must** correspond to only one value in the range. Functions, therefore, cannot be one-to-many.

1.3 Inverse functions

To return to the example of temperature, the inverse function reverses what was done by f – in other words it converts °C to °F. In building up the function f, two functions were used.

$$t \longrightarrow \boxed{\text{subtract 32}} \longrightarrow \boxed{\text{multiply by } \tfrac{5}{9}} \longrightarrow f(t)$$

To find the inverse function you need to 'undo' this:

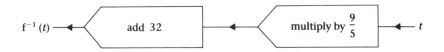

$$f^{-1}(t) \longleftarrow \boxed{\text{add } 32} \longleftarrow \boxed{\text{multiply by } \tfrac{9}{5}} \longleftarrow t$$

The inverse of f is denoted by f^{-1}. The flow diagram above shows that

$$f^{-1}(t) = \tfrac{9}{5}\,t + 32$$

As a quick check, note that

$$f(212) = 100 \quad \text{and} \quad f^{-1}(100) = 212$$

> (a) If $f(x) = x^2$, what are $f(-3)$ and $f(+3)$?
>
>   What is meant by $f^{-1}(9)$? Are there two possible answers?
>
> (b) What is meant by $\sqrt{x}$?
>
>   Does the same problem arise with $\sqrt[3]{x}$?

In order to avoid ambiguity, mathematicians take $\sqrt{x}$ to mean the **positive** square root of x, and $\sqrt[4]{x}$, $\sqrt[6]{x}$, $\sqrt[8]{x}$, . . ., to mean the positive fourth, sixth, eighth, . . . roots of x.

> $\sqrt{x}$ is the non-negative number whose square is x.

TASKSHEET 3 – Inverse functions (page 24)

The graphs of a function and its inverse function have reflection symmetry in the line $y = x$.

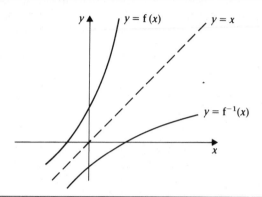

The inverse, f^{-1}, of a function f is itself a function only if f is one-to-one.

E X A M P L E   2

If $f(x) = (x - 3)^2 + 4$ $(x \geq 3)$,   find $f^{-1}(x)$.

S O L U T I O N

To find the inverse function, represent f by a flow chart showing the simpler functions which compose it.

Then reverse the flow chart.

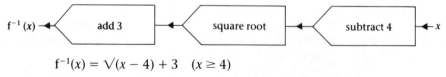

$$f^{-1}(x) = \sqrt{(x - 4)} + 3 \quad (x \geq 4)$$

Note that x is usually chosen to represent the input variable for the inverse function as well as the original function.

(a) Check that $f(7) = 20$ and $f^{-1}(20) = 7$.

(b) Explain the restrictions $x \geq 3$ and $x \geq 4$.

1.4 Rearranging formulas

The process of finding an inverse function is identical to that of rearranging a formula. In the temperature example,

$$f(t) = \tfrac{5}{9}(t - 32)$$

converts °F to °C, which could be written as

$$C = \tfrac{5}{9}(F - 32)$$

$$f^{-1}(t) = \tfrac{9}{5}t + 32$$

converts °C to °F, which could be written as

$$F = \tfrac{9}{5}C + 32$$

The formula for C in terms of F has been rearranged to give F in terms of C. The process can be seen as applying the same function to both sides of the formula and is often set out in this way:

$$C = \tfrac{5}{9}(F - 32) \qquad \text{Multiply both sides by } \tfrac{9}{5}$$

$$\tfrac{9}{5}C = F - 32 \qquad \text{Add 32 to both sides.}$$

$$\tfrac{9}{5}C + 32 = F$$

This approach may be used for finding inverse functions and is equivalent to the flow diagram as shown below.

$$C = \tfrac{5}{9}(F - 32)$$

$$\tfrac{9}{5}C = F - 32$$

$$\tfrac{9}{5}C + 32 = F$$

E X A M P L E   3

Make x the subject of the formula $y = (3x + 1)^2$.

S O L U T I O N

$$y = (3x + 1)^2 \qquad \text{Take the square root of each side.}$$

$$\pm\sqrt{y} = 3x + 1 \qquad \text{Subtract 1 from both sides.}$$

$$\pm\sqrt{y} - 1 = 3x \qquad \text{Divide both sides by 3.}$$

$$\frac{\pm\sqrt{y} - 1}{3} = x$$

TASKSHEET 4S – *Rearranging formulas (page 26)*

A particular difficulty arises with the flow chart method when the letter that is to be the subject of the formula appears more than once. A special strategy is then required, which is illustrated by the next example.

EXAMPLE 4

Find the inverse of the function

$$f(x) = \frac{x+1}{x+2} \quad (x \neq -2)$$

SOLUTION

Let $y = f(x)$, then rearrange to find x in terms of y.

$$y = \frac{x+1}{x+2}$$ Multiply both sides by $x + 2$.

$y(x+2) = x+1$ Multiply out the brackets.

$yx + 2y = x + 1$ Collect x terms together by subtracting $2y$ and then subtracting x from both sides.

$yx - x = 1 - 2y$ Factorise the left-hand side.

$x(y-1) = 1 - 2y$ Divide both sides by $y - 1$.

$$x = \frac{1-2y}{y-1}$$

Thus the inverse of the function which maps x to $\dfrac{x+1}{x+2}$ is

$$f^{-1}(y) = \frac{1-2y}{y-1}$$

x is conventionally chosen as the input variable and so it is usual to write

$$f^{-1}(x) = \frac{1-2x}{x-1}$$

What is the greatest possible domain of the function f^{-1}?

E X E R C I S E 2

1 Make x the subject of the following formulas.

(a) $y = \dfrac{5x - 3}{2}$ (b) $y = \dfrac{3}{4}(x - 5)$

(c) $y = (x - 5)^2 + 4$ (d) $y = \dfrac{1}{x - 3}$

2 Taking the formulas in question 1 as of the form $y = f(x)$, write down in each case the formula for $f^{-1}(x)$, stating also the greatest possible domain and range of f for which f^{-1} can be defined.

3 A major chemical company researching crop yields tries out a new pesticide. The results indicate that, per hectare, for a kg of pesticide the extra yield y kg of a crop is given by

$$y = \frac{900a}{2 + a}$$

(a) What is the formula which gives the amount, a kg, of pesticide needed to return an extra yield of y kg?

(b) Explain why the values of y will lie between 0 and 900.

4 Make x the subject of the formulas:

(a) $y = \dfrac{x - 1}{x + 1}$ (b) $y = \dfrac{2 - x}{x + 3}$

5 The graph of

$$y = \frac{x}{2x + 1}$$

is reflected in the line $y = x$. Find the equation of the image and use a graph plotter to check your answer.

(Hint: how are the graphs of $y = f(x)$ and $y = f^{-1}(x)$ related?)

6 If $f(x) = \dfrac{1 + x^2}{1 - x^2}$ $(x < -1)$ find $f^{-1}(x)$.

1.5 Parameters and functions

If a holidaymaker takes £x into her local bank, which offers an exchange rate of 10 francs to £1 and charges a commission of £4, the formula

$$f = 10(x - 4)$$

gives f, the number of francs that she will receive.

> (a) What would the formula be for an exchange rate of 9 francs to £1 and a commission of £7?
>
> (b) What would be the formula for an exchange rate of a francs to £1 and a commission of £b?

The formula $f = a(x - b)$ is of a more general kind than those met in the previous section and the roles of a and b are different from those of x and f. a and b can vary, but for any given function mapping x into f they will act as constants. They are called **parameters**.

$f = 10(x - 4)$ gives the value of £x in francs, at the given exchange rate. To find the number of pounds required to buy f francs you first need to rearrange the formula, giving

$$x = \frac{f}{10} + 4$$

Using the more general formula, the value of f francs in pounds is found by rearranging $f = a(x - b)$ to give

$$x = \frac{f}{a} + b$$

The same techniques used in finding the inverse of a function will be suitable if parameters replace numbers.

TASKSHEET 5 — Parametric formulas (page 27)

EXAMPLE 5

Make a the subject of the formula $s = ut + \frac{1}{2}at^2$.

SOLUTION

$s - ut = \frac{1}{2}at^2$ subtracting ut from both sides

$2s - 2ut = at^2$ multiplying both sides by 2

$\dfrac{2s}{t^2} - \dfrac{2u}{t} = a$ dividing both sides by t^2

$$a = \frac{2s}{t^2} - \frac{2u}{t}$$

EXERCISE 3

1 Make the variable shown in brackets the subject of the formula.

    (a) $P = aW + b$ (W) (b) $C = 2\pi r$ (r) (c) $s = \dfrac{n}{2}(a + l)$ (l)

    (d) $s = \dfrac{a}{1 - r}$ (r) (e) $\dfrac{1}{R} = \dfrac{1}{x} + \dfrac{1}{y}$ (x)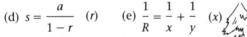

2

The driver of a car travelling at v m.p.h. sees an obstruction ahead of him and immediately applies the brakes. The distance, d feet, that the car travels from the time that the driver sees the obstruction until the car stops is given by

$$d = \frac{(v + 10)^2}{20} - 5$$

    (a) Find the stopping distance for a car travelling at

        (i) 30 m.p.h.   (ii) 50 m.p.h.   (iii) 70 m.p.h.

    (b) Rearrange the formula to find v in terms of d.

    (c) The driver sees an obstruction 250 feet ahead of him. What is the greatest speed at which he can be driving if he is to pull up before he reaches the obstruction?

1.6 Functions and transformations of graphs

You have seen that the graph of the inverse of a function is obtained by reflecting the graph of that function in the line $y = x$. You can now look at other transformations of graphs and find how the equations of the resulting graphs relate to those of the original graphs.

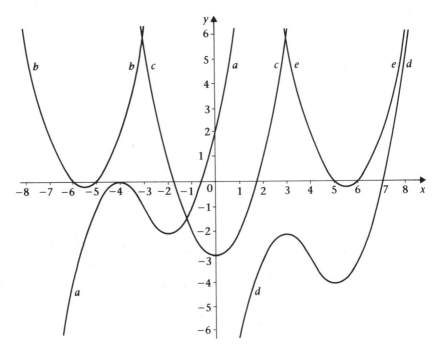

(a) Which of these graphs can be mapped onto other graphs in the diagram?

(b) What transformations would map

   (i) graph *b* onto graph *c*,

   (ii) graph *a* onto graph *d*,

   (iii) graph *b* onto graph *e*?

(c) Is there more than one possible answer to any of questions (i) to (iii)?

In the *Foundations* unit you saw that the image of the graph of $y = x^2$ under the translation $\begin{bmatrix} -2 \\ 3 \end{bmatrix}$ is the graph of $y = (x + 2)^2 + 3$. Using function notation, this can be expressed as

the image of $y = f(x)$ under a translation $\begin{bmatrix} -2 \\ 3 \end{bmatrix}$ is $y = f(x + 2) + 3$

In general:

The image of $y = f(x)$ under a translation $\begin{bmatrix} -p \\ q \end{bmatrix}$ is $y = f(x + p) + q$.

TASKSHEET 6 – Translations of graphs (page 29)

EXAMPLE 6

Find the image of the graph of $y = 5\sqrt{x}$ under a translation $\begin{bmatrix} 4 \\ 3 \end{bmatrix}$.

SOLUTION

Taking

$$f(x) = 5\sqrt{x} \quad \text{and} \quad p = -4, q = 3$$

then

$$f(x + p) + q = f(x - 4) + 3 = 5\sqrt{(x - 4)} + 3$$

so the image of

$$y = 5\sqrt{x}$$

is

$$y = 5\sqrt{(x - 4)} + 3$$

EXERCISE 4

Use translations of simple graphs to sketch the graphs of the following. In each case give the equation of the basic graph and the translation used.

1   $y = x^2 + 9$ 2 $y = (x - 1)^2$

3   $y = \dfrac{3}{x + \frac{1}{2}}$ 4 $y = x^3 - 2$

5   $y = 5(x - 3)^2 + 6$ 6 $y = x^2 + 2x$

1.7 **Combining transformations of graphs**

In section 1.6 you saw how translations of graphs changed their
equations. In this section you will consider other transformations
and combinations of transformations of graphs, together with their
effect on the general equation $y = f(x)$.

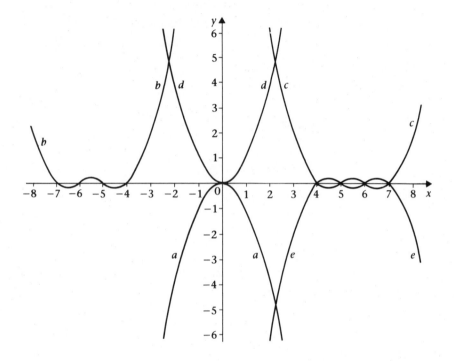

(a) Which of these graphs can be mapped onto other graphs in
the diagram?

(b) What transformations would map

(i) graph b onto graph c,

(ii) graph a onto graph d,

(iii) graph c onto graph e,

(iv) graph b onto graph e?

(c) Is there more than one possible answer to any of questions
(i) to (iv)?

TASKSHEET 7 – Combining transformations (page 30)

EXAMPLE 7

Find the image of $y = \dfrac{x^3}{4}$ after a translation of $\begin{bmatrix} -2 \\ -7 \end{bmatrix}$ followed by a reflection in the x-axis.

SOLUTION

Under a translation of $\begin{bmatrix} -2 \\ -7 \end{bmatrix}$, the image of $y = f(x)$ is $y = f(x + 2) - 7$.

So the image of $y = \dfrac{x^3}{4}$ is

$$y = \frac{(x + 2)^3}{4} - 7$$

Under a reflection in the x-axis, the image of $y = f(x)$ is

$$y = -f(x)$$

So the image of $y = \dfrac{(x + 2)^3}{4} - 7$ is

$$y = -\left\{ \frac{(x + 2)^3}{4} - 7 \right\}$$

i.e. $y = 7 - \dfrac{(x + 2)^3}{4}$

You have now seen the effects of translations and reflections in the axes. The general rules for these transformations are summarised below.

(a) **Translations:**   The graph of $y = f(x + p) + q$ is the image

of the graph of $y = f(x)$ after translation through $\begin{bmatrix} -p \\ q \end{bmatrix}$.

(b) **Reflections in the axes:**   The graph of $y = f(-x)$ is the image of the graph of $y = f(x)$ after it has been reflected in the y-axis. The graph of $y = -f(x)$ is the image of the graph of $y = f(x)$ after it has been reflected in the x-axis.

f is an even function if $f(-x) = f(x)$. The graph of such a function is symmetric about the y-axis.

f is an odd function if $f(-x) = -f(x)$. The graph of such a function has rotational (half-turn) symmetry about the origin.

E X E R C I S E 5

1 For each of the following pairs of graphs, the equation of one graph is given.
Find the equation of the other.

Use the graph plotter to check your answers.

(a)

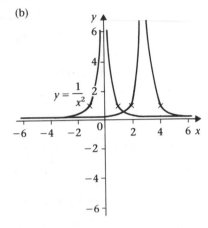

(b)

(c)

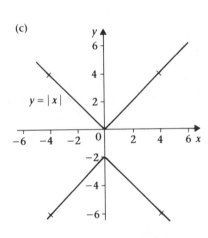

(d)

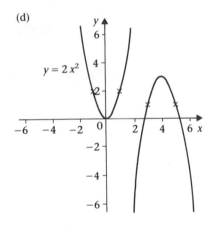

(e)

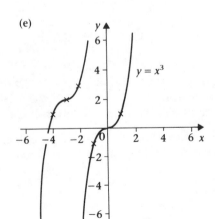

(f)

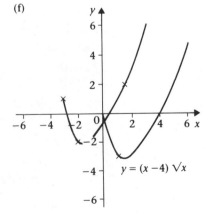

2   Find the images of the graphs of the following functions under the transformations given.

(a) $y = \dfrac{1}{x}$,   reflection in the x-axis followed by a translation

   through $\begin{bmatrix} -6 \\ -7 \end{bmatrix}$

(b) $y = 3x - 7$,   reflection in the y-axis followed by a reflection in the x-axis

(c) $y = \dfrac{1}{x^2}$,   translation through $\begin{bmatrix} 2 \\ -3 \end{bmatrix}$ followed by a reflection in the x-axis

---

After working through this chapter you should:

1   be able to combine functions;

2   be able to find the inverse of a function;

3   be able to rearrange formulas;

4   be able to find the images of graphs after

   (a) translation,

   (b) reflections in the axes,

   (c) reflection in the line $y = x$;

5   be able to use your knowledge of transformations to help you sketch graphs;

6   understand the terms domain, range, one-to-one, even, odd, as applied to functions.

Functions of functions

1 The functions f and g given by $f(x) = x^2$ and $g(x) = 3x + 1$ can be described by the following flow charts.

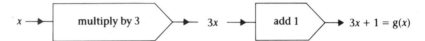

(a) (i) What is f(4)?   (ii) What is g(16)?

(b) If the output from $f(x)$ is used as input to $g(x)$, you can write $g(f(x))$. What is $g(f(4))$?

(c) Write down   (i) $g(f(2))$ (ii) $g(f(-3))$ (iii) $f(g(-2))$

(d) Draw a flow chart to describe the composite function $gf(x)$ and hence find a formula for $gf(x)$.

(e) Check whether your formula is correct by substituting a few simple numbers in $gf(x)$ and in your formula.

(f) Now find a formula for $fg(x)$.

2 (a) Use the ideas above to find $gf(x)$ and $fg(x)$ for

   (i) $f(x) = \dfrac{1}{x}$, $g(x) = x - 3$ (ii) $f(x) = 2x$, $g(x) = \sqrt{x}$

   (iii) $f(x) = x + 5$, $g(x) = x - 9$ (iv) $f(x) = 10 - x$, $g(x) = 10 - x$

   (v) $f(x) = \dfrac{1}{x}$, $g(x) = \dfrac{1}{x}$

   (b) Comment on the cases where $fg(x) = gf(x)$.

3 Each of the expressions below is of the form $fg(x)$ where $f(x) = 1 - x^2$. What is $g(x)$ in each case?

   (a) $1 - (x + 2)^2$ (b) $1 - x^4$ (c) $1 - \dfrac{1}{x^2}$ (d) $1 - x$

4 Each of the expressions below is of the form $fg(x)$ where $g(x) = x^3$. What is $f(x)$ in each case?

   (a) $x^3 + 8$ (b) x^6 (c) $3x^3 + 1$ (d) $\dfrac{12}{x^3}$ (e) x (f) $4x^3 - x^6$

Functions of functions

1 ff(x) means the function f applied twice to x; this is often written as $f^2(x)$.

If each of the expressions below is f(x), write down an expression for $f^2(x)$ in each case.

(a) $x + 2$ (b) x^2 (c) $2x - 3$ (d) x (e) $\sin x$ (f) $\dfrac{1}{x}$

2 If f(x) = $x - 3$ and g(x) = x^2, it is possible to combine these functions in many ways.

(a) Explain why $(x - 3)^2 - 3 = $ fgf(x).

(b) Express each of the following as combinations of f and g.

(i) $x^2 - 3$ (ii) $(x^2 - 3)^2$ (iii) $x - 6$ (iv) $x^8 - 3$ (v) $(x - 3)^4 - 6$

3 Using s(x) = $\sin x$ and q(x) = x^2, distinguish clearly between:

(a) $\sin^2 x$, i.e. $(\sin x)^2$ (b) $\sin x^2$, i.e. $\sin (x^2)$ (c) $\sin \sin x$, i.e. $\sin (\sin x)$

4 In each case, find fg(x) and gf(x), and then determine the set of values for which fg(x) = gf(x).

(a) f(x) = x^2,   g(x) = $x + 3$ (b) f(x) = $x - 5$,   g(x) = $x + 2$

(c) f(x) = $2x - 1$,   g(x) = $3x + 1$ (d) f(x) = $\dfrac{1}{x}$,   g(x) = x^3

(e) f(x) = $2x + 1$,   g(x) = $\frac{1}{2}(x + 1)$ (f) f(x) = $\sqrt{x}$,   g(x) = $x - 1$

5 Four functions, e, f, g and h, are defined by

$$e(x) = x \qquad f(x) = -x \qquad g(x) = \frac{1}{x} \qquad h(x) = -\frac{1}{x}$$

Then fg(x) = f $\left(\dfrac{1}{x}\right) = -\dfrac{1}{x} \Rightarrow$ fg = h

Complete the following table, where each entry is one of e, f, g or h.

		Second function			
		e	f	g	h
First function	e	e	f		
	f	f	e	*	
	g				
	h				

* The function to be entered here is fg, i.e. h.

Inverse functions

For a function f, if the inverse f^{-1} is also a function the situation must be like this.

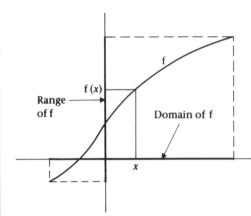

Since f is a function, any vertical line cuts the graph once only.

Since f^{-1} is a function, any horizontal line cuts the graph once only.

1 (a) What is $f^{-1}(f(x))$?

  (b) Explain why the domain of f is the range of f^{-1}.

  (c) Sketch the graph of a function whose inverse is not a function.

  (d) If both f and f^{-1} are functions, explain why f must be a one-to-one function.

2 For each of the following functions, obtain a formula for the inverse.

  (a) $f(x) = 3x + 5$ (b) $g(x) = x^2 - 7$

  (c) $h(x) = (x - 7)^2$ (d) $r(x) = \sqrt{x} + 6$

3 (i) For each function in question 2, choose a suitable domain so that the inverse is also a function and plot on the same axes (which should have equal scales) the graphs of the function, its inverse and $y = x$.

  (ii) What simple transformation will map the graph of $y = f(x)$ onto the graph of $y = f^{-1}(x)$?

4 The graph of

  (a) $f(x) = (x + 5)^2 - 3$ (b) $f(x) = 3(2x - 1)$

  is reflected in the line $y = x$. Find the equation of the image.

5 (a) Investigate the sequences:

  (i) $x_{n+1} = \dfrac{1}{x_n}$ (ii) $x_{n+1} = -x_n$

  for various different values of x_1 in each case.

(b) What is the inverse of:

(i) $f(x) = \dfrac{1}{x}$, the reciprocal function, and

(ii) $f(x) = -x$, the 'change sign' or 'multiply by -1' function?

Why do you think these functions are called self-inverse? Sketch the graphs of the two functions and explain how they are related to what you observed in question 3.

EXAMPLE

Find the inverse of $f(x) = \dfrac{1}{1-x}$ $(x = 1)$

SOLUTION

Flow chart for f:

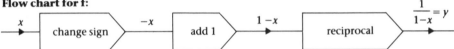

Its reverse for f^{-1}:

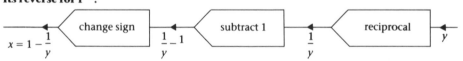

$$f^{-1}(y) = 1 - \frac{1}{y}$$

As a quick check, note that: $f(3) = -0.5$, $f^{-1}(-0.5) = 3$.

The letter y can be changed for any other and it is usual to write $f^{-1}(x) = 1 - \dfrac{1}{x}$.

6   Find the inverse of each of the functions f defined as follows.

(a) $f(x) = \dfrac{1}{2x + 1}$ $(x \neq -\frac{1}{2})$

(b) $f(x) = 12 - x$ (or $-x + 12$) $(x \in \mathbb{R})$

(c) $f(x) = \dfrac{1}{x} - 1$ $(x \neq 0)$

(d) $f(x) = \dfrac{8}{(x + 1)^2}$ $(x > -1)$

(e) $f(x) = \sqrt{(1 - x^2)}$ $(0 \leqslant x \leqslant 1)$

(f) $f(x) = 4 - (x - 2)^2$ $(x \geqslant 2)$

Which of these functions are self-inverse? What are the equations of the lines of symmetry of the graphs of the self-inverse functions?

Rearranging formulas

1 Complete the steps to make x the subject of the formula

$$y = 5(x - 7)^2$$

$\_\_\_ = (x - 7)^2$ divide both sides by 5

$\_\_\_ = (x - 7)$ find the square root of each side

$\_\_\_ = x$ add 7 to both sides

2 Make x the subject of the formula

(a) $y = 3x^2 - 7$ (b) $y = \dfrac{(2x + 1)^2}{9}$ (c) $y = 3\sqrt{x} - 1$

3 Complete the steps to find x in terms of y if

$$y = \frac{3}{x} - 4$$

$\_\_\_ = 3 - 4x$ multiply both sides by x

$\_\_\_ = 3$ add $4x$ to both sides to collect terms in x together

$(\_\_\_)x = 3$ factorise the left-hand side

$$x = \frac{3}{\_\_\_}$$

4 Make x the subject of the formula

(a) $y = 2 - \dfrac{1}{x}$ (b) $y = \dfrac{3}{x^2}$ (c) $y = 5 + \dfrac{1}{2\sqrt{x}}$

Parametric formulas

1 If a metal rod is heated, the length increases according to the equation

$$l = l_0(1 + \alpha t)$$

where l is the final length, l_0 is the initial length, t is the increase in temperature and α is the coefficient of expansion of the rod.

Complete the missing steps to find α in terms of l, l_0 and t.

$$l = l_0(1 + \alpha t)$$

$$\Rightarrow \ \_\_\_\_\_ \ = 1 + \alpha t$$

$$\Rightarrow \ \_\_\_\_\_ \ = \alpha t$$

$$\Rightarrow \ \_\_\_\_\_ \ = \alpha$$

Hence find α if a steel rod of length 1 metre expands to a length of 1.004 m when heated through 230 °C.

2 Einstein's famous equation $E = mc^2$ gives the energy released by a mass m, where c is the speed of light. Rearrange this equation to find c in terms of E and m.

3 If a body of mass m moving with velocity u is later observed to be moving with velocity v then the change in kinetic energy of the body is given by

$$E = \tfrac{1}{2} m v^2 - \tfrac{1}{2} m u^2$$

Rearrange this formula to give v in terms of E, m and u.

4 A pendulum consists of a light steel rod with a heavy metal disc attached to the end. The time, T, taken for the pendulum to swing through a complete cycle is given by

$$T = 2\pi \sqrt{\left(\frac{l}{g}\right)}$$

where l is the length of the pendulum and g is a constant.

Complete the following steps to find l in terms of T and g.

$$\_\_\_\_\_ \ = \sqrt{\left(\frac{l}{g}\right)} \qquad \text{[square both sides]}$$

$$\Rightarrow \ \_\_\_\_\_ \ = \frac{l}{g}$$

$$\Rightarrow \ \_\_\_\_\_ \ = l$$

For a grandfather clock, $T = 2$ and $g = 9.81$ in SI units. The equation then gives a value for l in metres. Find this value.

5 (a) Show that the surface area of a solid cylinder of radius r and height h is

$$S = 2\pi r(r + h)$$

(b) Rearrange the formula $S = 2\pi r(r + h)$ to give h in terms of S and r.

6 In rearranging formulas a student proceeds as follows. Simplify her working in order to arrive at more elegant solutions.

(a) The volume V of a cone of radius r and height h is

$$V = \frac{1}{3}\pi r^2 h \quad \Rightarrow \quad \frac{V}{\frac{1}{3}\pi} = r^2 h$$

$$\Rightarrow \quad r = \sqrt{\frac{\left(\dfrac{V}{\frac{1}{3}\pi}\right)}{h}}$$

(b) The total interest £I on £P invested at r% for n years is given by

$$I = \frac{Prn}{100} \quad \Rightarrow \quad I \times 100 = Prn$$

$$\Rightarrow \quad r = \frac{\left(\dfrac{I \times 100}{P}\right)}{n}$$

7 Locate and correct the errors in the following.

(a) The current I flowing in a circuit consisting of a resistance R and n batteries of voltage E and internal resistance r each is given by

$$I = \frac{nE}{R + nr} \quad \Rightarrow \quad IR = \frac{nE}{nr} \quad \Rightarrow \quad R = \frac{E}{Ir}$$

(b) The kinetic energy E of a body of mass m moving with speed v is

$$\Rightarrow E = \frac{1}{2}mv^2$$

$$\Rightarrow v = \frac{\sqrt{(\frac{1}{2}m)}}{E}$$

Translations of graphs

1   The function f is defined by $f(w) = w^4$.

   (a) Write down the expressions $f(x)$, $f(x) + 2$ and $f(x + 3)$, then plot the graphs of $y = f(x)$, $y = f(x) + 2$ and $y = f(x + 3)$ on the same screen.

   (b) What simple transformations would transform the graph of $y = f(x)$ onto the graph of

       (i) $y = f(x) + 2$ (ii) $y = f(x + 3)$?

2   The function g is defined by $g(u) = \dfrac{1}{u}$.

   (a) Write down the expressions $g(x)$, $g(x + 4)$ and $g(x + 4) + 3$, then plot the graphs of $y = g(x)$, $y = g(x + 4)$ and $y = g(x + 4) + 3$ on the same screen.

   (b) What simple transformations would transform the graph of $y = g(x)$ onto the graph of

       (i) $y = g(x + 4)$ (ii) $y = g(x + 4) + 3$?

3

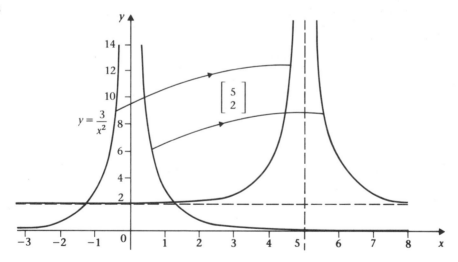

The graph of $y = \dfrac{3}{x^2}$ is translated through $\begin{bmatrix} 5 \\ 2 \end{bmatrix}$ as shown above. Suggest an equation for the new curve. Check your answer by plotting the graph of your equation.

4   By completing the square, rewrite $y = x^2 + 4x + 3$ in the form $y = (x + p)^2 + q$.

   What transformation will map the graph of $y = x^2$ onto the graph of $y = x^2 + 4x + 3$? Check your answer by plotting both graphs on the same screen.

Combining transformations

1 (a) If $f(w) = w^2 - w$, write down expressions for $f(x)$, $f(-x)$ and $-f(x)$ and draw their graphs.

   (b) (i) What transformation will map $y = f(x)$ onto $y = f(-x)$?

       (ii) What transformation will map $y = f(x)$ onto $y = -f(x)$?

   (c) For any function f, will the transformations found in (b) always be the same? Give reasons for your answer.

2 (a) $f(x) = x^4 - 2x^3$. The graph of $y = f(x)$ is reflected in the *x*-axis. Use the ideas of question 1 to find the equation of the new graph. Plot both graphs to check your answer.

   (b) The original graph is now reflected in the *y*-axis. Write down the equation of the new graph. Plot the graph of your equation to check your answer.

3 (a) If $f(x) = 3x^2 - x^4$, write down $f(-x)$. Plot the graphs of $f(x)$ and $f(-x)$. Explain what occurs.

   (b) If $f(x) = x^3 - 5x$, write down $f(-x)$ and $-f(x)$. Plot the graphs of $f(x)$, $f(-x)$ and $-f(x)$. Explain what occurs.

If $f(-x) = f(x)$, then f is called an **even** function and its graph has line symmetry in the *y*-axis.

If $f(-x) = -f(x)$, then f is called an **odd** function and its graph has rotational symmetry about the origin.

4 Classify the following functions f as odd, even or neither.

   (a) $f(x) = \dfrac{3}{x^2}$ (b) $f(x) = 2x^5 - 3x^3$ (c) $f(x) = x^3 + 2$

5 Classify the following functions f as odd, even or neither.

(a)

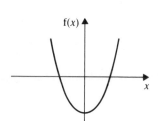

(b)

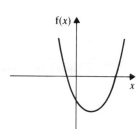

(c)

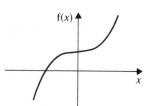

(d)

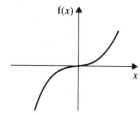

(e)

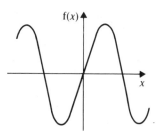

(f)

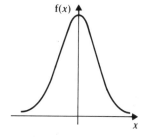

6 $f(x) = x^2 + 3x - 2$. The graph of $y = f(x)$ is first reflected in the x-axis and then the new curve is reflected in the y-axis.

(a) Find the equations of these two new curves and plot the three graphs to check your answers.

(b) How could you have transformed the first curve onto the third using a single transformation?

7 $f(x) = 2x^2 - \dfrac{1}{x}$

The graph of $y = f(x)$ is first reflected in the y-axis and then translated through $\begin{bmatrix} 4 \\ 3 \end{bmatrix}$.

Find the equation of the final curve. Check your answer by using the graph plotter.

2 Circular functions

2.1 Rotation

A cowboy is sitting on the top rail of a fence spinning a lasso, to which is tied a handkerchief. The handkerchief is moving in a circle of radius 1 metre and its height above the top rail is changing continuously. To find its position at any moment, a simple mathematical model is needed.

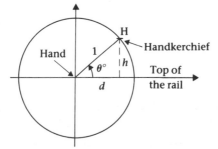

Define $(\cos \theta°, \sin \theta°)$ to be the coordinates of H, in metres.

So $h = \sin \theta°$, where $\theta°$ is the angle through which the handkerchief has turned from the horizontal position.

(a) Explain why $(\cos \theta°, \sin \theta°)$ may be defined as the coordinates of H and why $h = \sin \theta°$.

(b) Is this definition still appropriate when

(i) θ is greater than 360,   (ii) θ is negative?

(c) What must the cowboy do with the lasso to obtain a negative angle?

By considering the height, h metres, of the handkerchief above the rail as θ varies, the sine curve can be obtained. The cosine curve is obtained by considering the horizontal distance from the cowboy's hand, d metres.

 TASKSHEET 1S – Sin θ and cos θ° (page 47)

The sine and cosine functions are both **periodic** – that is, they repeat themselves after a certain interval known as the **period**. In the case of both sine and cosine the period is 360°.

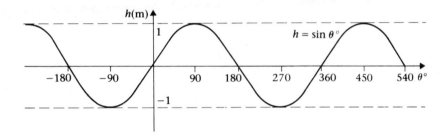

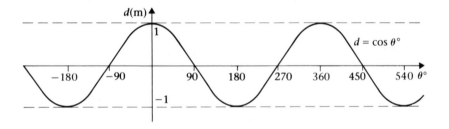

EXERCISE 1

1 (a) Use your calculator to give the value of sin 50°.

 (b) Write down, from the sine graph, six other angles which have the same sine as 50°.

2 (a) Use your calculator to find cos 163°.

 (b) Write down, from the cosine graph, five other angles which have the same cosine as 163° and which lie in the range $-360 \leq \theta \leq 720$.

3 (a) Use your calculator to find sin 339°.

 (b) Write down, from the sine graph, five other angles which have the same sine as 339° and which lie in the range $-360 \leq \theta \leq 720$.

2.2 **Transformations**

A

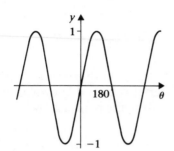

B

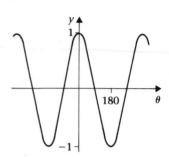

C

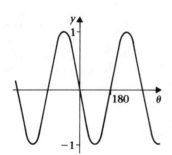

D

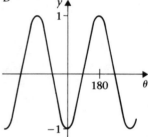

Which of the graphs A, B, C, D is obtained if

(a) A is reflected in the θ-axis,

(b) B is reflected in the θ-axis,

(c) A is reflected in the y-axis,

(d) B is reflected in the y-axis,

(a) What are the equations of the four graphs?

(b) What do the questions above tell you about the relationship between

(i) $\sin(-\theta)°$ and $\sin \theta°$, (ii) $\cos(-\theta)°$ and $\cos \theta°$?

(c) Are the sine and cosine functions odd, even, or neither odd nor even?

TASKSHEET 2 – Transformations (page 49)

Tasksheet 2 has shown that

starting with $y = \sin x°$,

$y = \sin (x + c)° + d$ is obtained by a translation of $\begin{bmatrix} -c \\ d \end{bmatrix}$.

$y = a \sin x°$ is obtained by a one-way stretch parallel to the y-axis which changes the **amplitude** of the function from 1 to a.

$y = \sin bx°$ is obtained by a one-way stretch parallel to the x-axis which changes the **period** of the function from 360 to $\left(\dfrac{360}{b} \right)$.

$y = \sin (bx + c)°$ is obtained by a stretch of $\dfrac{1}{b}$ followed by a translation of $\dfrac{-c}{b}$, called a **phase shift** of $\dfrac{-c}{b}$.

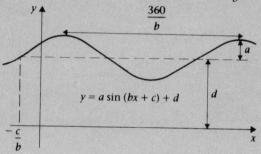

Are the effects of these transformations on circular functions consistent with their effects on polynomial functions?

E X A M P L E   1

(a) For $y = 3 \cos(6\theta + 180)°$, what are the amplitude, period and phase shift? Sketch the graph.

S O L U T I O N

Amplitude 3.
Period 60.
Phase shift $-30°$.

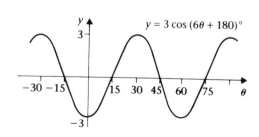

35

EXERCISE 2

1   Suggest suitable equations for the following graphs. Check your answers using a graph plotter.

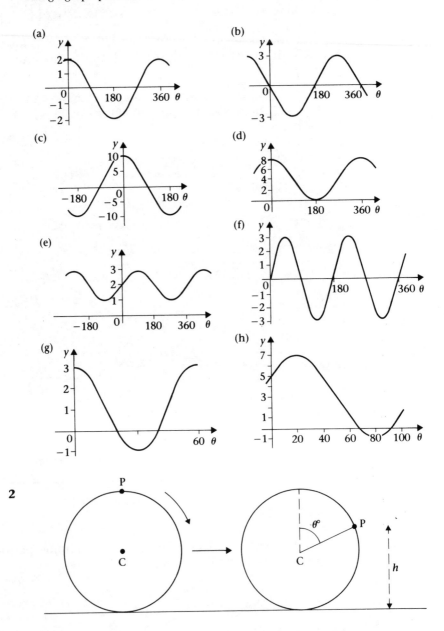

(a)

(b)

(c)

(d)

(e)

(f)

(g)

(h)

2

A wheel of radius 0.2 metres rolls along a straight horizontal line. Initially, a spot P on the rim is directly over the centre C. After turning through $\theta°$, the height of the spot P is h metres. Find an equation for h in terms of θ and sketch the graph of h against θ.

2.3 Modelling periodic behaviour

The sine and cosine functions are ideal for modelling many situations which are periodic. As you will see, the input to a sine or cosine function need not be an angle.

EXAMPLE 2

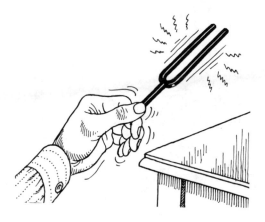

When a tuning fork is struck, each prong vibrates at a frequency of 256 Hz (cycles per second) with a maximum displacement at the tip of 0.3 mm.

(a) Sketch a graph to show the displacement of the tip of a prong with time.

(b) Assuming that this is a sine graph, express d, the displacement in mm, as a function of t, the time in seconds from the start of the motion.

SOLUTION

(a) Assume the initial displacement is 0.3

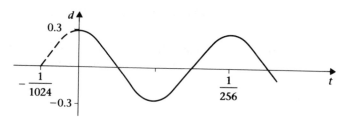

(b) $d = a \sin (bt + c)°$

Amplitude: $a = 0.3$

Period: $\dfrac{360}{b} = \dfrac{1}{256} \Rightarrow b = 92\,160$

Phase shift: $\dfrac{-c}{b} = -\dfrac{1}{1024} \Rightarrow c = 90$

So $d = 0.3 \sin (92\,160t + 90)°$

TASKSHEET 3 — Applications (page 50)

EXERCISE 3

1 As the Moon circles the Earth, its gravitational force causes tides. The height of the tide can be modelled by a sine or cosine function.

(a) Assuming an interval of 12 hours between successive high tides,

   (i) sketch the graph of the height if it is 5.7 metres at low tide and 7.3 metres at high tide;

   (ii) use the graph to help express the height of the tide, h metres, as a function of the time t hours after high tide.

(b) Express h as a function of t if h is 3.6 at low tide and 4.9 at high tide.

2 The times for sunset at four-weekly intervals over a year are as follows:

Jan. 2	16:03	July 16	21:10
Jan. 30	16:45	Aug. 13	20:27
Feb. 27	17:36	Sep. 10	19:26
Mar. 26	18:24	Oct. 8	18:22
Apr. 23	20:11	Nov. 5	16:26
May. 21	20:55	Dec. 3	15:54
June 18	21:21		

Plot this data on a graph and, making any necessary adjustments, find a suitable function to model the data approximately.

2.4 Inverse trigonometric functions

In studying periodic behaviour it is often useful to be able to solve problems involving the inverse functions. For example, a student who believes that his intellectual bio-rhythm is governed by the equation

$$I = \sin\left(\frac{360t}{33}\right)^{\circ}$$

may wish to know on what days his value for I is greater than 0.9. In order to do this he would need to solve the equation

$$\sin\left(\frac{360t}{33}\right)^{\circ} = 0.9$$

Before you can solve equations like this, you need to be able to solve equations of the form $\sin x^{\circ} = a$.

(a) Use your calculator to find a solution to the equation $\sin x^{\circ} = 0.6$.

(b) How many more solutions can you find to this equation?

(c) Why is the inverse of f, where $f(x) = \sin x^{\circ}(x \in \mathbb{R})$, **not** a function?

If $\sin a^{\circ} = b$, then $a^{\circ} = \sin^{-1} b$, where $\sin^{-1} b$ means 'the angle whose sine is b'.

In order to ensure that $\sin^{-1}$ is a function, you need to restrict the image set to those values given by a calculator. These values are known as the **principal values**.

For $\sin^{-1} x$ the principal values lie in the range $-90° \le \sin^{-1} x \le 90°$.

Use your calculator to find the range of principal values of $\cos^{-1} x$.

TASKSHEET 4E — Inverse functions (page 52)

EXAMPLE 3

(a) Find the principal value of $\cos^{-1}(-0.25)$.

(b) Solve $\cos x° = -0.25$ for $-360 \le x \le 360$.

SOLUTION

(a) A calculator gives $\cos^{-1}(-0.25)$ as $104.5°$, which is the principal value.

(b) A graph shows there are four solutions. Angles having the same cosine are found using the symmetry of the graph. They are:

A $-360 + 104.5 = -255.5°$
B $-104.5°$
C $104.5°$
D $360 - 104.5 = 255.5°$

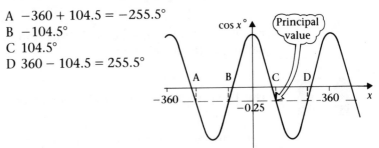

sin^{-1} and cos^{-1} both have domain $\{x \in \mathbb{R} : -1 \le x \le 1\}$.
If they are taken as functions, their ranges are restricted to the sets of principal values

$$-90° \le \sin^{-1} x \le 90° \quad \text{and} \quad 0° \le \cos^{-1} x \le 180°$$

EXERCISE 4

1 Give the principal values of the following.

(a) $\sin^{-1} 0.2$ (b) $\cos^{-1} 0.9$ (c) $\sin^{-1}(-0.36)$

(d) $\cos^{-1}(-0.74)$ (e) $\sin^{-1}(1)$ (f) $\cos^{-1}(-1)$

2 Solve the following equations, giving solutions in the range $-360 \le x \le 720$.

(a) $\sin x° = 0.3$ (b) $\cos x° = 0.8$ (c) $\cos x° = -0.3$

(d) $\sin x° = -0.5$ (e) $\cos x° = -1$ (f) $3 \sin x° = 1$

3 Use a graph plotter to sketch the graphs of

(a) $y = \sin^{-1} x$ (b) $y = \cos^{-1} x$

2.5 Solving equations

Suppose that the height of the tide, h metres, at a harbour entrance is modelled by the function

$$h = 2.5 \sin 30t° + 5$$

where t is the number of hours after midnight.

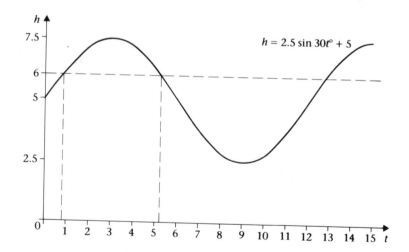

$$h = 2.5 \sin 30t° + 5$$

(a) When is the height of the tide 6 m?

(b) If a boat can only enter and leave the harbour when the depth of water exceeds 6 m, for how long each day is this possible?

EXAMPLE 4

A girl is sitting on a big wheel which rotates once every 30 seconds. When the wheel begins to rotate for the ride, she is sitting in the position shown in the picture and marked A on the diagram. The diameter of the wheel is 16 m.

Her height y metres above the lowest point of the wheel t seconds later is given by

$$y = 8 + 8 \sin (12t + 30)°$$

At what times is she

(a) 15 metres above the ground;

(b) at the highest point?

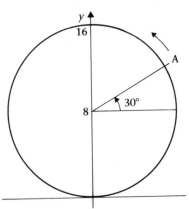

SOLUTION

(a) When $y = 15$, you need to solve the equation

$$8 + 8 \sin (12t + 30)° = 15$$

$\Rightarrow \qquad 8 \sin (12t + 30)° = 7$

$\Rightarrow \qquad \sin (12t + 30)° = 0.875$

Now solve $\sin x° = 0.875$, where $x = 12t + 30$.

The calculator gives $x = 61.0$ so the possible solutions are

$$x = 61.0, \ 180 - 61.0, \ 360 + 61.0, \ldots$$

$$\Rightarrow \ 12t + 30 = 61.0, \ 119.0, \ 421.0, \ 479.0, \ldots$$

$$\Rightarrow \ t = 2.6, \ 7.4, \ 32.6, \ 37.4, \ldots$$

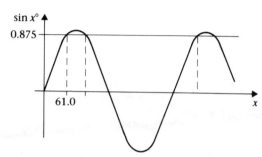

(b) At the highest point, $y = 16$, so you have to solve the equation

$$8 + 8 \sin (12t + 30)° = 16$$

$$\Rightarrow \qquad 8 \sin (12t + 30)° = 8$$

$$\Rightarrow \qquad \sin (12t + 30)° = 1$$

Now solve $\sin x° = 1$, where $x = 12t + 30$.

This time there is only a single solution for each cycle and you do not need a calculator to tell you that the basic solution is $x = 90$. So the possible solutions are

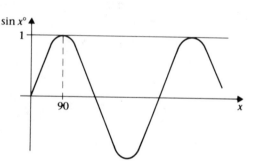

$$x = 90, \ 360 + 90, \ 720 + 90, \ 1080 + 90, \ldots$$

$$\Rightarrow \ 12t + 30 = 90, \ 450, \ 810, \ 1170, \ldots$$

$$\Rightarrow \qquad t = 5, \ 35, \ 65, \ 95, \ldots$$

The function $\sin (12t + 30)°$ has a period of $\dfrac{360}{12} = 30$ so if $t = a$ is a solution then so is $t = 30\,n + a$, where n is any integer.

TASKSHEET 5S — Solving equations (page 53)

EXERCISE 5

1 Find the values of t in the range $0 \le t \le 60$ which satisfy the following equations.

(a) $8 \sin 10t° = 5$ (b) $4 - 7 \cos (t + 35)° = 0$

(c) $3 + 4 \sin (8t - 21)° = 0$ (d) $10 \cos \frac{1}{2}t° = 9$

2 The height above ground of a chair in a big wheel is given by

$$h = 5.6 - 4.8 \cos 6t°$$

where t is the time measured in seconds from the instant when the chair is at the lowest point. For how many seconds during one complete revolution is the chair more than 9 metres above ground level?

3 If the height of the tide is h metres at time t hours, where

$$h = 5 + 2.5 \sin 30t°$$

find all the times in the first 24 hours when the height is

(a) 6.7 metres; (b) 4.5 metres.

4 A cowboy ties a handkerchief to a lasso which he then spins so that the height in metres of his handkerchief above the ground after t seconds is given by

$$h = 2 + 1.5 \sin 500t°$$

Find at what times the height of the handkerchief above the ground is

(a) 2.75 metres; (b) 2 metres; (c) 3.5 metres.

2.6 Tan $\theta°$

Whilst sine and cosine are the most commonly used, they are not the only periodic functions. Another important function is the tangent function.

TASKSHEET 6S — Tan $\theta°$ (page 54)

A tennis umpire, U, is watching a rally between two players. The ball, B, is hit straight down the court from P to Q over the centre of the net, C.

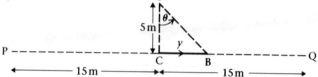

(a) What is (i) length y, (ii) angle CUQ?

(b) Sketch a graph to show how y varies with θ as the ball travels (i) from C to Q, (ii) from P to Q.

(c) Using the sides of a right-angled triangle, show that if $0 \leqslant \theta < 90$ then

$$\tan \theta° = \frac{\sin \theta°}{\cos \theta°}$$

(d) What is the greatest possible domain for tan?

(e) Find a suitable set of principal values for $\tan^{-1} x$.

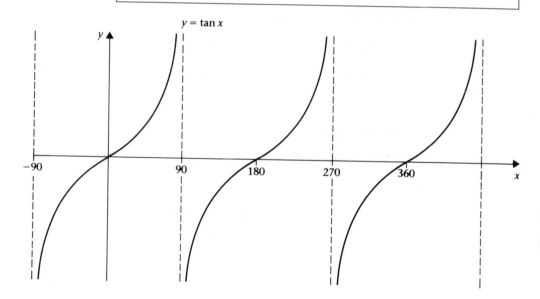

$y = \tan x$

$$\tan x = \frac{\sin x}{\cos x} \ (\cos x \neq 0)$$

$\tan x$ is an odd function; $\tan(-x) = -\tan x$.

The graph of $y = \tan x$ can be transformed into the graph of $y = a \tan(bx + c) + d$ in the same way as the graph of $y = \sin x$ is transformed into the graph of $y = a \sin(bx + c) + d$.

EXERCISE 6

1 Find the principal values of

  (a) $\tan^{-1} 1$ (b) $\tan^{-1}(-6)$ (c) $\tan^{-1} 0$

2 Sketch the graphs of

  (a) $y = \tan 2x°$ (b) $y = \tan(x + 45)°$

3 Solve the equations for values of x in the range $0 \leq x \leq 360$.

  (a) $\tan x° = 3$ (b) $5 \tan(2x + 30)° = 4$

  (c) $\tan^2 x° = 1$ (d) $4 \sin x° = 3 \cos x°$

After working through this chapter you should be able to:

1 define sin, cos, tan and their inverses;

2 sketch the graph of a circular function such as

  $$y = a \sin(bx + c)$$

3 obtain solutions to equations of the form

  $$a \cos(bx + c) = d$$

  in a specified range;

4 apply circular functions in modelling periodic behaviour.

Sin $\theta°$ and cos $\theta°$

You will need the axes given on Datasheet 1: *Sin $\theta°$ and cos $\theta°$*.

1 (a)

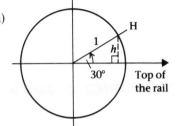

$h = \sin \ldots$

$(\theta, h) = (30, \ldots)$

Plot this point on the axes.

(b) Work out and plot the point (θ, h) for the following values of θ. (Give all values on this tasksheet to 2 significant figures.)

    (i) $\theta = 45$
    $h =$
    $(\theta, h) = (45, \quad)$

    (ii) $\theta = 60$
    $h =$
    $(\theta, h) = (60, \quad)$

    (iii) $\theta = 0$
    $h =$
    $(\theta, h) = (0, \quad)$

    (iv) $\theta = 90$
    $h =$
    $(\theta, h) = (90, \quad)$

2 (a)

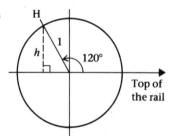

$h = \sin \ldots$

$(\theta, h) = (120, \ldots)$

Plot this point on the axes.

(b) Work out and plot the point (θ, h) on the axes when

    (i) $\theta = 135$
    (ii) $\theta = 150$
    (iii) $\theta = 180$

3 (a)

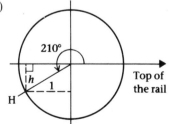

$h = \sin \ldots$

$(\theta, h) = (210, \ldots)$ Watch the sign!

Plot this point on the axes.

(b) Work out and plot (θ, h) on the axes when

    (i) $\theta = 225$
    (ii) $\theta = 240$
    (iii) $\theta = 270$

4 (a)

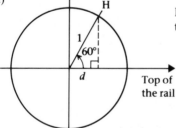

Find h and plot the point $(\theta, h) = (300, h)$ on the axes.

300°

Top of the rail

1

H

(b) Work out and plot the point (θ, h) on the axes when

(i) $\theta = 315$ (ii) $\theta = 330$ (iii) $\theta = 360$

5 The cowboy's lasso does not stop, so the handkerchief will keep going round. Work out and plot the point (θ, h) on the axes when θ takes the following values:

390, 405, 420, 450, 480, 495, 510, 540

6 Draw a smooth curve through the points plotted to give the graph of sin $\theta°$.

7 (a)

H

Find d and plot the point $(\theta, d) = (60, d)$ on the axes.

1

60°

d

Top of the rail

(b) Work out and plot the point (θ, d) on the axes when θ takes each of the following values:

30, 45, 90, 120, 135, 150, 180, 210, 225, 240, 270, 300, 315 330, 360, 390, 405, 420, 450, 480, 495, 510, 540

(c) Draw a smooth curve through the points plotted to give the graph of cos $\theta°$.

Transformations

1 Use a graph plotter, working in degrees, to plot the graph of

$$y = \sin \theta°$$

Investigate the graph of $y = a \sin \theta°$ for various values of a, including negative values, and describe the transformations involved. a is called the **amplitude** of the function.

2 (a) Investigate $y = \sin b\theta°$ for various values of b and comment on the significance of the factor b.

(b) What is the period of $\sin b\theta°$ in terms of b?

3 Investigate $y = \sin (\theta + c)° + d$ for various values of c and d and describe the transformations involved.

4 Investigate

(a) $y = \cos b\theta°$ (b) $y = \cos (b\theta + c)°$

for various values of b and c and carefully describe the transformations involved.

5

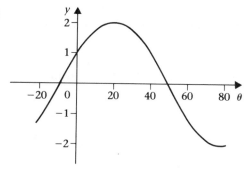

The diagram shows a part of the graph of

$$y = a \sin (b\theta + c)°.$$

Find a, b and c.

6 Describe fully a sequence of transformations which maps the graph of

$$y = \cos \theta°$$

onto the graph of

$$y = a \cos (b\theta + c)° + d$$

where a, b, c and d may take any values. Illustrate your conclusions with appropriate diagrams.

Applications

1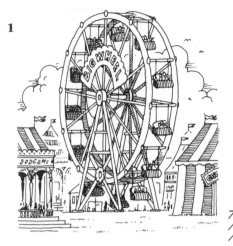

A big wheel has a radius of 4.8 m and a seat in the lowest position is 0.8 m above ground level. One complete revolution takes 60 seconds.

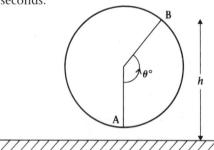

(a) If a seat starts from the bottom, in position A and if after t seconds it has turned through an angle $\theta°$, express θ in terms of t.

(b) Draw a rough sketch to show how the height in metres, h, will vary with (i) θ, (ii) t. (There is no need to perform any detailed calculations.) In each case, suggest a possible formula for h.

(c) Plot a graph of the first part of the motion by completing the following table of values of h for various values of θ.

θ	0	30	60	90	120	150	180
h							

(d) Repeat part (c), but this time using t as the variable.

t	0	5	10	15	20	25	30
h							

You may have noticed that a subtle change has occurred in this example. Until now sin and cos have been used exclusively with **angles** as input. In part (d), however, the input to the function was t. There is no reason why, having drawn the basic graphs of the circular functions, you should not use **any variable** you choose as input. The following questions illustrate this further.

2 (a)

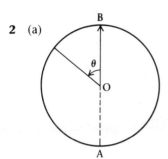

A wave machine in a swimming pool comprises a cylinder of radius 2 m which rotates at 1 revolution every 10 seconds. The cylinder starts with the bar, B, uppermost and has rotated through an angle $\theta°$ after t seconds. A is a fixed point just beneath the cylinder. Express θ in terms of t.

(b) Hence, write down the height of the bar above (i) O, (ii) A, after t seconds.

3

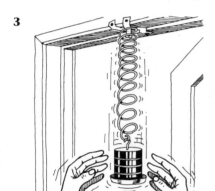

A mass oscillates up and down at the end of a spring. The unstretched length of the spring is 12 cm, and it is extended to 14.5 cm and released. One complete oscillation takes one second. Sketch a graph to show the length of the spring as a function of time. Assuming that this is a cosine graph, express l, the length in centimetres, as a function of t, the time in seconds from the start of the motion.

4 The 'science' of bio-rhythms is based on the belief that an individual's behaviour is governed by three cycles which begin at birth. The physical cycle (P) with a period of 23 days governs such things as strength, confidence and aggression. The emotional cycle (E) with a period of 28 days affects feelings, creativity and cooperation; whilst the intellectual cycle (I), period 33 days, covers intelligence, concentration, memory and quickness of mind.

Critical days in an individual's behaviour occur when the graph of a cycle crosses the time axis.

Each cycle of the physical curve may be modelled by a sine wave using the equation

$$P = \sin\left(\frac{360t}{23}\right)°$$

(a) Suggest suitable models for the other two cycles.

(b) Calculate your current values for P, E and I.

(c) When is your next critical day for each of the three cycles?

(d) On what days of your life are all three cycles critical?

Inverse functions

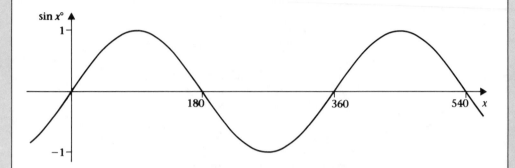

1 (a) Use your calculator to find a solution of $\sin x° = 0.4$.

   (b) Use the graph above to find three more solutions in the range $0 \le x \le 540$.

   (c) Write down two solutions in the range $3600 \le x \le 3960$.

   (d) Write down two solutions in the range $360n \le x \le 360 (n + 1)$.

   (e) Does your formula apply if n is negative?

Your solution to question 1(d) is known as the **general solution** of the equation. It is possible to write the general solution in a rather more elegant form, as question 2 demonstrates.

2 (a) Find a solution, p, of $\sin x° = 0.5$ in the range $0 \le x \le 90$.

   (b) Two more solutions are $180 - p$ and $360 + p$. Write down the next two in the same form.

   (c) Write down the 20th and 21st terms of the sequence starting p, $180 - p$, $360 + p$.

   (d) Write down the nth term. (Hint: $(-1)^n$ equals $+ 1$ if n is even, -1 if n is odd.)

3 Find the general solutions of

   (a) $\sin x° = 0.7$ (b) $\sin x° = -0.7$ (c) $\cos x° = 0.7$

4 Find $\sin^{-1} x + \cos^{-1} x$ for various values of x and explain your result.

Solving equations

This tasksheet is designed to emphasise and give extra practice in the methodology needed to solve equations involving sine and cosine functions.

1 To solve the equation $4 \cos x° = 3$:

(a) Write down the value of $\cos x°$;

(b) Use your calculator to give one solution for x;

(c) Sketch the graph of $y = \cos x°$.

(d) (i) Mark on the graph the solution from the calculator.

   (ii) Mark on the graph the other solution between 0 and 360.

   (iii) Write down the value of this other solution.

2 Find all the solutions between 0 and 360 for the following equations, illustrating your answers with sketch graphs.

(a) $\cos x° = 0.56$ (b) $\sin x° = -0.23$ (c) $\cos x° = -0.5$

3 Find all the solutions between -180 and 180 for these equations, illustrating your answers with sketch graphs.

(a) $\sin x° = 0.65$ (b) $\cos x° = -0.38$ (c) $\sin x° = -0.47$

4 Find all the solutions between 0 and 360 for the following equations.

(a) $3 \sin x° = 2$ (b) $5 \cos x° + 2 = 0$ (c) $2 \cos x° + 5 = 0$

5 Copy and complete the solution of $5 \sin (3t + 40)° = 4$.

$$5 \sin (3t + 40)° = 4 \implies \sin (3t + 40)° = \ldots$$

This is equivalent to $\sin x° = \ldots$, where $x = 3t + 40$

From the calculator, $x = \ldots$

So (using a sketch of the graph of $\sin x°$) six possible solutions are

$$x = \ldots, \quad \ldots, \quad \ldots, \quad \ldots, \quad \ldots, \quad \ldots$$

$$\implies 3t + 40 = \ldots, \quad \ldots, \quad \ldots, \quad \ldots, \quad \ldots, \quad \ldots$$

$$\implies \quad t = \ldots, \quad \ldots, \quad \ldots, \quad \ldots, \quad \ldots, \quad \ldots$$

6 Solve these equations for values of t between 0 and 360.

(a) $\sin 2t° = 0.7$ (b) $2 \cos 3t° = 1$ (c) $3 \cos (0.5t + 20)° = 2$

Tan $\theta°$

1 (a)  Draw a diagram such as the one on the left. By taking measurements from the diagram, complete this table.

θ	10	20	30	40	50	60
$\tan \theta$						

(b) Check your values using a calculator and extend the table up to $\theta = 80$.

(c) What happens when $\theta = 90$?

2 (a) Use your calculator to complete the following table.

θ	0	15	30	45	60	75	90
$\sin \theta°$							
$\cos \theta°$							
$\dfrac{\sin \theta°}{\cos \theta°}$							

(b) Find $\tan \theta°$ for the values of θ given in the table.

What is the relationship between $\dfrac{\sin \theta°}{\cos \theta°}$ and $\tan \theta°$?

Does your relationship hold when $\theta = 90$?

(c) Assuming that the relationship just found holds for θ in all four quadrants, sketch the graph of $y = \tan \theta°$ for $-360 < \theta < 360$.

3 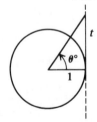 Relate the tan function to the length of a tangent to a circle, using this figure. (This explains the name of the function.)

Explain how you can interpret $\tan \theta°$ as the length of a tangent when

(a) $-90 < \theta < 0$ (b) $90 < \theta < 270$

3 Growth functions

3.1 Exponential growth

Under favourable circumstances some organisms exhibit a
particular type of unrestricted growth. The graph shows the growth
of a number of bacteria starting with roughly 3000 at time $t = 0$
(hours).

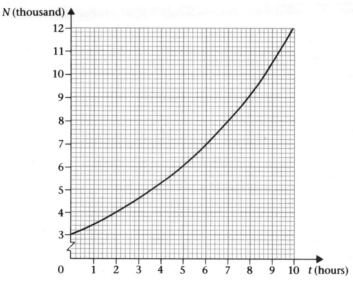

Estimate, using the graph, the times when the numbers of
bacteria were

(a) 4000, 8000   (b) 5000, 10000

Estimate when the numbers of bacteria were

(c) 24000   (d) 1500

Describe the feature of the graph which enabled you to make
these estimates.

> Growth is called **exponential** when there is a constant, called
> the **growth factor**, such that during each unit time interval
> the amount present is multiplied by this factor.

E X A M P L E   1

The graph shows the growth
of world population from
1650 to 1950. Is the growth
exponential?

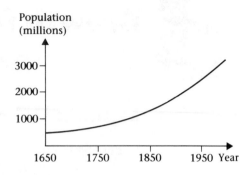

S O L U T I O N

The populations in 1650, 1750, 1850 and 1950 were approximately
500 million, 700 million, 1300 million and 2500 million.

> Find the growth factors over successive hundred-year intervals. Is
> the growth exponential?

Exponential decay occurs when the growth factor is less than 1.

E X A M P L E   2

A scientist was analysing the decay of a radioactive form of lead,
lead-214. The mass of lead-214 remaining in a particular sample of
lead was measured to be as follows:

Time (minutes)	0	1	2	3	4	5	6	7	8
Mass (kg)	3.127	3.047	2.969	2.894	2.820	2.748	2.678	2.609	2.542

Was the radioactive lead decaying exponentially?

S O L U T I O N

In the first minute, the growth factor is $\dfrac{3.047}{3.127} = 0.974$.

As you can verify, the growth factors in succeeding minutes are all
0.974.
The lead decayed exponentially (the constant growth factor is less
than 1).

EXERCISE 1

1 To attract new investors, a construction company published its pre-tax profit figures for the previous ten years.

Profit before tax
(millions of pounds)

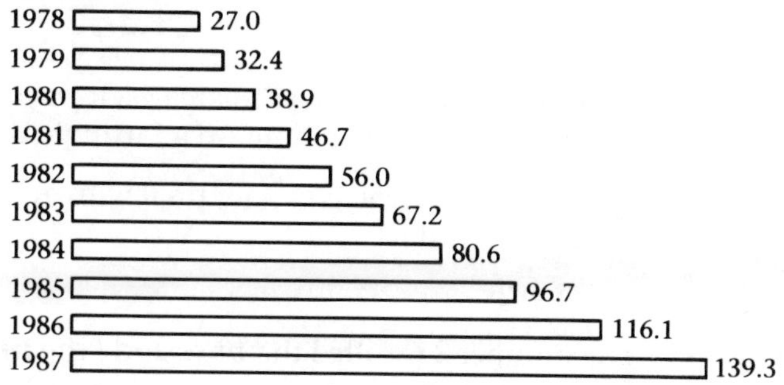

1978 ☐ 27.0
1979 ☐ 32.4
1980 ☐ 38.9
1981 ☐ 46.7
1982 ☐ 56.0
1983 ☐ 67.2
1984 ☐ 80.6
1985 ☐ 96.7
1986 ☐ 116.1
1987 ☐ 139.3

Was the growth of profits exponential?

2 In 1984, £5000 was deposited in a fixed interest building society account. The amount in the account increased as shown below.

1985	1986	1987	1988	1989
£5450	£5940.50	£6475.15	£7057.91	£7693.12

What was the interest rate? Was the growth exponential?

3 A girl's annual pocket money is £50 plus £10 for each year of her age. Does her pocket money increase exponentially with age?

4 The following table shows the population of Latin America over a period of 24 years.

Year	1950	1954	1962	1966	1974
Population (millions)	164	183	227	254	315

Is this exponential growth? Justify your answer.

5 A capacitor is an electronic component which can store charge.

(a) A capacitor is initially charged to 9 volts. It is discharged across a particular circuit, the voltage dropping by one volt each second.

(b) In another circuit, the voltage would have dropped by one quarter of its value each second.

Are either of the above examples of exponential decay? Find the growth factors, if appropriate.

3.2 Indices

| 1 week ago | Now | In 1 week | In 1½ weeks | In 2 weeks |

A culture of algae doubles in area each week. Now it covers $1\,\text{cm}^2$, so in a week it will cover $2\,\text{cm}^2$, in a fortnight $4\,\text{cm}^2$, etc.

The growth of algae is exponential with growth factor 2. In t weeks the area, A, will be

$$A = 2^t$$

The number 2 is called the **base** and t the **index** (plural: indices).

> Using the context of algal growth, explain what meaning can be given to the expression 2^t when t is 0, -1 and $1\frac{1}{2}$.

The tasksheet introduces definitions and laws for powers of 2 and other base numbers.

TASKSHEET 1 — Indices (page 69)

For any **positive** number a and **any** numbers p, q:

$$a^0 = 1$$

$$a^{-p} = \frac{1}{a^p}$$

$$a^p \times a^q = a^{p+q}$$

$$a^p \div a^q = a^{p-q}$$

$$(a^p)^q = a^{pq}$$

If n is non-zero

$$a^{\frac{1}{n}} = \sqrt[n]{a}$$

> Are these laws true when a is
>
> (a) negative, (b) 1, (c) 0, (d) a fraction?

EXAMPLE 3

By using a combination of several laws of indices, evaluate $8^{-\frac{2}{3}}$.

SOLUTION

$$8^{-\frac{2}{3}} = \frac{1}{8^{\frac{2}{3}}} = \frac{1}{(8^{\frac{1}{3}})^2}$$

$$= \frac{1}{(\sqrt[3]{8})^2} = \frac{1}{2^2}$$

$$= \frac{1}{4}$$

State which law is used in each stage of the calculation.

EXERCISE 2

1 Express the following as single powers of 2.

(a) $2^2 \times 2^3$ (b) 2×2^9 (c) $2^{12} \div 2^7$ (d) $(2^5)^3$

2 Simplify the following:

(a) $x^2 \times x^3$ (b) $a \times a^9$ (c) $d^{12} \div d^7$ (d) $(b^5)^3$

3 Evaluate:

(a) 3^{-2} (b) 10^{-3} (c) $3^{-2} \times 3^5$ (d) $5^2 \div 5^{-1}$

4 Simplify:

(a) $y^3 \times y^{-5}$ (b) $c^3 \div c^{-2}$ (c) $x^{-5} \times x^5$ (d) $(x^{-2})^{-3}$

5 Evaluate these, checking your answers using the x^y or $x^{\frac{1}{y}}$ key on your calculator.

(a) $4^{\frac{1}{2}}$ (b) $25^{-\frac{1}{2}}$ (c) $25^{-\frac{3}{2}}$ (d) $1000000^{\frac{1}{3}}$ (e) $0.01^{\frac{1}{2}}$

6 Use your calculator to solve the equation $2^t = 10$ by trial and improvement, correct to two decimal places.

TASKSHEET 2S   –   Laws of indices (page 71)

3.3 Growth factors

In section 3.2 you considered the growth function with equation $y = 2^x$. In many fields of study it can be useful to find equations which closely model given data. For example, the population figures for England and Wales from 1841 to 1901 are as follows:

Year	1841	1851	1861	1871	1881	1891	1901
Population, P millions	15.9	17.9	20.1	22.7	26.0	29.0	32.5

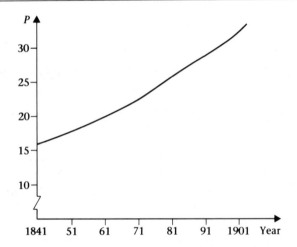

If you could fit an equation to such data, then you could make reasonable estimates for populations in years when a census was not taken and you could also project the figures beyond the years for which data is available. However, great care must be taken in making such projections because changes in conditions dramatically alter population trends.

How can you decide if the population figures given can be closely approximated using a growth function?

How can you estimate the growth factor?

Some of the properties of the equations and graphs of growth functions are investigated on the next tasksheet.

TASKSHEET 3 – Ka^x (page 72)

> The general growth function has an equation of the form
> $y = Ka^x$, where K and a are constants. K is the value of y when
> x is zero and a is the growth factor.

E X A M P L E   4

Model the population data for England and Wales with an equation
for P in terms of t, the number of years after 1841.

S O L U T I O N

Assuming the growth is exponential, $P = K \times a^t$. $K = 15.9$, the initial
value and, since $32.5 = 15.9 \times a^{60}$ the annual growth factor can be
estimated by

$$\left(\frac{32.5}{15.9}\right)^{\frac{1}{60}} \approx 1.012$$

The equation is then

$$P = 15.9 \times 1.012^t$$

A check on the suitability of this model can be made by comparing
tabulated values of the original data and populations predicted by
the equation.

t	0	10	20	30	40	50	60
P		15.9	17.9	20.1	22.7	26.0	29.0	32.5
15.9×1.012^t	15.9	17.9	20.2				

> Complete the table above and decide if the model is reasonable.
>
> What does the model predict for the population of England and
> Wales in 1990? Comment on your answer.

EXERCISE 3

1 A colony of bacteria has a growth factor of 6 per hour. Initially there are 400 bacteria.

(a) After how many hours will there be 14 400 bacteria?

(b) When will there be 1 000 000 bacteria?

(c) Write down an expression for the number of bacteria t hours after the start.

2 The compound interest on a savings account is 8% per annum.

(a) What is the growth factor?

(b) Explain why the number, n, of years before an initial investment of £4000 grows to £5000 is given by $1.08^n = 1.25$.

(c) Find an approximate value for n.

3 A radioactive element, bismuth-210, was observed every few days, and the mass remaining was measured.

The following figures were obtained:

No. of days from start of experiment	0	2	3	6	7	10
Mass (kg)	10	7.57	6.57	4.34	3.77	2.48

(a) Estimate the growth factor.

(b) Write down an equation for M, the mass of bismuth remaining, in terms of t, the number of days from the start of the experiment.

(c) Check how well your equation models the data.

(d) How much will remain after 3 weeks?

(e) What is the half-life of bismuth-210 (i.e. after how many days does only half of the original amount remain), to the nearest whole day?

3.4 Logarithms

The graph shows the growth of aquatic plants starting with an initial surface coverage of $1\,m^2$.

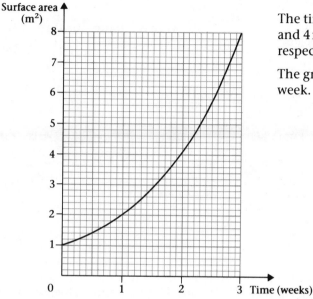

The time taken to reach $2\,m^2$ and $4\,m^2$ are 1 and 2 weeks respectively.

The growth factor is 2 per week.

(a) Write down the surface area A after t weeks.

(b) How long does it take before the surface area is $5\,m^2$?

The exponential equation expresses A as a function of t. Often though, you require the **inverse function**, i.e. t in terms of A. This inverse function is called the **logarithm of A to base 2**, written as $\log_2 A$.

From the graph the area is $8\,m^2$ after 3 weeks, i.e. $8 = 2^3$. Conversely, it takes 3 weeks before the area is $8\,m^2$, i.e. $3 = \log_2 8$.

(a) Estimate $\log_2 3$ from the graph.

(b) What is (i) $\log_2 32$, (ii) $\log_{10} 1000$, (iii) $\log_3 27$?

(c) How can you sketch the graph of $y = \log_2 x$?

TASKSHEET 4 — Properties of logs (page 73)

You have obtained the following results.

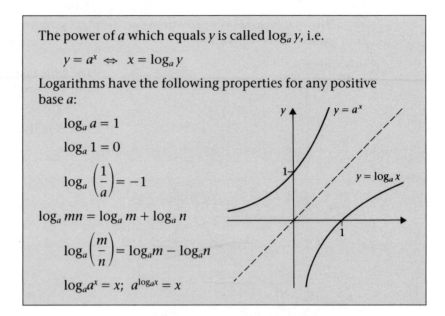

The power of a which equals y is called $\log_a y$, i.e.

$$y = a^x \iff x = \log_a y$$

Logarithms have the following properties for any positive base a:

$$\log_a a = 1$$

$$\log_a 1 = 0$$

$$\log_a \left(\frac{1}{a}\right) = -1$$

$$\log_a mn = \log_a m + \log_a n$$

$$\log_a \left(\frac{m}{n}\right) = \log_a m - \log_a n$$

$$\log_a a^x = x; \quad a^{\log_a x} = x$$

In pre-calculator days, tables of logarithms were used to help perform various calculations. Part of a table of logarithms to base 10 is given below. From the table, $\log_{10} 1.351 = 0.1306$ and so on.

●	1	2	3	4	5	6	7	8	9	1	2	3	4	5	6	7	8	9
1.0	.0000	0043	0086	0128	0170	0212	0253	0294	0334	0374	4	8	12	17	21	25	29	33	37
1.1	.0414	0453	0492	0531	0569	0607	0645	0682	0719	0755	4	8	11	15	19	23	27	30	34
1.2	.0792	0828	0864	0899	0934	0969	1004	1038	1072	1106	3	7	10	14	17	21	24	28	31
1.3	.1139	1173	1206	1239	1271	1303	1335	1367	1399	1430	3	6	10	13	16	19	23	26	29
1.4	.1461	1492	1523	1553	1584	1614	1644	1673	1703	1732	3	6	9	12	15	18	21	24	27
1.5	.1761	1790	1818	1847	1875	1903	1931	1959		2014	3	6	8	11	14	17	20	22	25
1.6	.2041	2068	2095	2122	2148	2175	2201				3	5	8	11			18	21	24

> How can you use the table of logarithms shown above to calculate $1.17 \div 1.091$?

In 1615, the Scottish mathematician John Napier discussed the idea of using logarithms with the Oxford professor Henry Briggs. Two years later, Briggs published his first table of logarithms (to 14 decimal places!) and after much further work published his *Arithmetica Logarithmica* in 1624.

Nowadays logarithms are pre-programmed into calculators and computers but originally their calculation involved considerable hard work and ingenuity. 'Log' is by convention taken to mean $\log_{10}$, and you will therefore find that the $\boxed{\log}$ key on calculators evaluates logarithms to the base 10.

EXERCISE 4

1 You have seen that

$$2^3 = 8 \Rightarrow \log_2 8 = 3$$

From these equations with indices, form equations using logarithms.

(a) $3^2 = 9$ (b) $4^{-3} = \frac{1}{64}$ (c) $(0.5)^{-2} = 4$

(d) $(\frac{1}{8})^{-\frac{1}{3}} = 2$ (e) $27^{\frac{2}{3}} = 9$

2 Write down the values of

(a) $\log_2 (\frac{1}{4})$ (b) $\log_5 125$ (c) $\log_7 (\frac{1}{7})$ (d) $\log_8 (\frac{1}{4})$

3 Simplify:

(a) $\log_3 9 + \log_3 27 - \log_3 81$ (b) $\log_5 15 - \log_5 3$ (c) $2 \log_7 \sqrt{7}$

4 Sketch, on the same axes, $y = \log_{10} x$, $y = \log_{10} 2x$ and $y = \log_{10} 3x$. How are the graphs related? Use the laws of logs to explain this relationship.

5 (a) Use the log tables on the previous page to calculate 1.05×1.267.

(b) Use the properties of logs to write down $\log_{10} 10.5$ and $\log_{10} 1267$. Hence use log tables to find 10.5×1267.

6 The notation 4! means $4 \times 3 \times 2 \times 1$ and is read as '4 factorial'. If $\log_5 4! = 1.9746$, write down $\log_5 5!$.

7 A colony of bacteria doubles every hour. Explain why the time t hours for the colony to increase in size 1000-fold is given by $2^t = 1000$. Express t as a logarithm to base 2 and explain why $9 < t < 10$. Use a numerical method to find t to two decimal places.

3.5 The equation $a^x = b$

In answering the problem in exercise 4 about a colony of bacteria you used a numerical method to solve the equation

$$2^t = 1000$$

Problems concerning growth often lead to such equations, in which the unknown occurs as an index. It will be useful to develop a more direct method for dealing with them.

Suppose that a radioactive isotope decays by 10% each year.

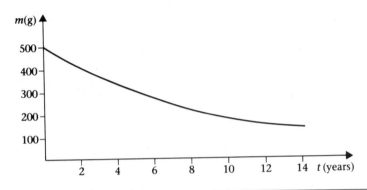

(a) Initially there is 500 g of the isotope. Find an expression for the amount t years later.

(b) The half-life of the isotope is the time taken for the amount present to decrease by 50%. Use the graph to estimate this half-life.

(c) What equation must be solved to find the half-life more precisely?

Equations of the form

$$a^x = b$$

can be solved by a numerical method. There is, however, a more direct way of solving such equations.

TASKSHEET 5 – $a^x = b$ (page 75)

If $a > 0$,

$$\log a^p = p \log a$$

EXAMPLE 5

Find the half-life of the radioactive isotope considered in the discussion point.

SOLUTION

$$500 \times 0.9^x = 250$$
$$\Rightarrow \qquad 0.9^x = 0.5 \quad \text{(divide both sides by 500)}$$
$$\Rightarrow \qquad \log 0.9^x = \log 0.5 \quad \text{(take logs of both sides)}$$
$$\Rightarrow \qquad x \log 0.9 = \log 0.5 \quad \text{(using the property of logs above)}$$
$$\Rightarrow \qquad x = \frac{\log 0.5}{\log 0.9} \approx 6.58$$

The half-life is approximately 6.58 years.

EXERCISE 5

1 Solve for x:

(a) $2^x = 32$ (b) $9^x = 243$ (c) $8^x = 256$

(d) $3^x = 10.05$ (e) $5^x = 9.2$ (f) $2.073^x = 7.218$

2 Explain how you could have obtained the answers to 1(a), 1(b) and 1(c) without using a calculator.

3 A colony of bacteria has a growth factor of 3.7 per hour and initially there are 250 bacteria.

(a) Write down an expression for the number of bacteria after t hours.

(b) Find the time (to the nearest minute) after which there are 10000 bacteria.

4 A capacitor is discharging with a growth factor of 0.9 per second. After how long will there be $\frac{1}{5}$ of the original charge? (Give your answer in seconds, to 2 d.p.)

5 In question 2 of exercise 3, you found that the number, n, of years needed for an investment of £4000 to grow to £5000 at 8% per annum compound interest was given by $1.08^n = 1.25$. Find n using logarithms.

6 In 1980, the population of Africa was 470 million and growing at a rate of 2.9% per annum. In what year will its population reach one thousand million according to this model?

7 In 1980, the population of China was 995 million and growing at a rate of 1.4% per annum. After how many years will the population of China equal that of Africa?

After working through this chapter you should:

1 recognise data which exhibits exponential growth;

2 understand the relationship between logarithms and indices;

3 be able to draw the graph of the logarithmic function;

4 be able to use the laws of indices and logarithms;

5 be able to model data using the equation $y = Ka^x$;

6 be able to solve equations of the form $a^x = b$.

Indices

The area, A, covered by an algal growth is initially $1\,\text{cm}^2$. The growth increases exponentially with time, t, in such a way that $A = 2^t$, where t is measured in weeks.

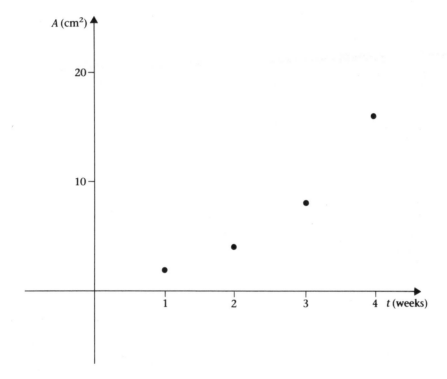

So far 2^t has been defined only when t is a positive whole number. It is nevertheless sensible to join the points on the graph with a smooth curve.

1 (a) Explain why, for whole number powers,

(i) $2^m 2^n = 2^{m+n}$ (ii) $2^m \div 2^n = 2^{m-n}$

(b) Simplify $(2^m)^n$.

2 From your graph, find 2^0 and interpret 2^0 in terms of growth of algae.

3 (a) What was the area of algae a week before measurements started? How would you define 2^{-1}?

(b) Use the same approach to define

(i) 2^{-2} (ii) 2^{-3} (iii) 2^{-n}

4 You do not have to restrict yourself to doubling. Suggest values for

(a) 3^{-2} (b) 5^0 (c) 10^{-6} (d) a^0 (e) a^{-n}

You need to check that the laws of question 1 are still being obeyed.

5 (a) Use the laws to simplify $2^{-4}2^{-3}$.

(b) Express 2^{-4} and 2^{-3} as fractions.

(c) Multiply the two fractions in (b) to check that the answer in (a) fits in with the laws of indices.

(d) Verify that the laws hold for

　(i) $2^{-3} \times 2^0$　(ii) $2^{-1} \times 2$　(iii) $2^{-4} \div 2^{-3}$　(iv) $2 \div 2^{-3}$

6 Decide which of the following are equal.

(a) $\left(\dfrac{1}{2}\right)^3$ (b) $\dfrac{1}{2^3}$ (c) 8 (d) 2^{-3} (e) $\dfrac{1}{8}$ (f) 3^{-2}

7 (a) If $2^{\frac{1}{2}}$ is to obey the laws, what must $\left(2^{\frac{1}{2}}\right)^2$ equal?

(b) What is $(\sqrt{2})^2$?

How will you define

(c) $2^{\frac{1}{2}}$ (d) $2^{\frac{1}{3}}$ (e) $2^{\frac{1}{n}}$ (f) $a^{\frac{1}{n}}$?

8 Find (a) $9^{\frac{1}{2}}$ (b) $8^{\frac{1}{3}}$ (c) $64^{\frac{1}{4}}$ (d) $81^{0.5}$

9 (a) Explain why $4^{\frac{p}{q}} = \left(4^{\frac{1}{q}}\right)^p$.

(b) Find the value of (i) $8^{\frac{2}{3}}$, (ii) $16^{\frac{3}{4}}$.

10 Check the laws of indices using the graph and your calculator. For example, on your calculator find $\sqrt{2}$ and $2^{0.5}$.

Read off from your graph the value of A when $t = 0.5$.

You should experiment with various bases and both signs of indices.

Laws of indices

1 Express the following as single powers of 2.

(a) $2^5 \times 2^7$ (b) $2^{10} \div 2^7$ (c) $2^5 \div 2^4$ (d) $2^3 \div 2$

(e) $2^4 \div 2^4$ (f) $(2^3)^2$ (g) $(2^2)^3$ (h) $(2^4)^4$

2 Simplify the following.

(a) $y^5 \times y^7$ (b) $b^{10} \div b^7$ (c) $c^5 \div c^4$ (d) $x^3 \div x$

(e) $y^4 \div y^4$ (f) $(a^3)^2$ (g) $(a^2)^3$ (h) $(b^4)^4$

3 Evaluate:

(a) 2^{-5} (b) 5^{-1} (c) 4^{-2} (d) $2^{-3} \times 2^{-1}$

(e) $5^2 \times 5^{-4}$ (f) $8^0 \times 8^{-2}$ (g) $2^{-3} \div 2^{-4}$ (h) $3^{-4} \div 3$

4 Simplify:

(a) $x^{-3} \times x^4$ (b) $a^3 \div a^5$ (c) $b^2 \times b^{-2}$ (d) $(d^{-2})^3$

(e) $x^{-5} \div x^5$ (f) $(y^3)^{-1}$ (g) $(a^5)^0$ (h) $x^3 \times x^{-2} \times x$

5 Evaluate:

(a) $8^{\frac{1}{3}}$ (b) $16^{-\frac{1}{4}}$ (c) $27^{\frac{2}{3}}$ (d) 3^{-2}

(e) $16^{\frac{3}{4}}$ (f) $1000^{-\frac{1}{3}}$ (g) 25^0 (h) $100^{\frac{3}{2}}$

(i) $(\frac{1}{4})^{-2}$ (j) $1^{\frac{3}{5}}$ (k) $(\frac{1}{2})^{-3}$ (l) 0.1^{-4}

(m) $81^{\frac{3}{4}}$ (n) $125^{-\frac{2}{3}}$ (o) $1000000^{\frac{1}{3}}$ (p) $0.01^{-\frac{3}{2}}$

Ka^x

You have seen that $y = a^x$ may be used as a model for exponential growth. In this tasksheet you will see how, by changing the function to Ka^x, you can model **any** exponential data.

1 (a) Investigate the graph of $K \times 2^x$ for various values of K. What is the significance of the factor K?

   (b) What is the significance of K if $y = K \times a^x$?

2 (a) If $y = a^t$, what is the **initial** value of y, i.e. the value of y when $t = 0$?

   (b) If $y = K \times a^t$ what is the initial value of y?

3 Investigate the graph of $K \times (\frac{1}{2})^x$ for various value of K. What is the significance of the factor K?

4 Use the ideas developed in questions 1–3 to sketch the graphs of

   (a) $y = 5 \times 3^t$ (b) $y = 2 \times (\frac{1}{3})^t$ (c) $y = \frac{1}{2} \times 5^t$ (d) $y = 2 \times (\frac{1}{5})^t$

   Check your answers using a graph plotter.

5 The population P of the UK was estimated at 1.5 million in 1066 and 6.1 million in 1700. Assume that an exponential growth model is appropriate and that t years after 1066, $P = Ka^t$.

   (a) Write down the value of K.

   (b) Use the data for the population in 1700 to explain why

   $$a = \left(\frac{6.1}{1.5}\right)^{\frac{1}{634}}$$

   Evaluate this to 5 decimal places.

   (c) Use this model to estimate the population of the UK in 1990.

   (d) Comment on the model.

6 In an electronic circuit, the voltage V across a capacitor drops from 15 volts to 6 volts in 12 seconds. Assuming that the process is one of exponential decay, write down a formula for V in terms of t, the time in seconds from the start.

Properties of logs

$$y = 2^x \iff x = \log_2 y$$

1 Find (a) $\log_2 64$ (b) $\log_2 \frac{1}{8}$ (c) $\log_2 2$ (d) $\log_2 \sqrt{2}$

Just as you can find the logarithm of a number to base 2, you can find logarithms to any positive base. The power of a which equals y is called $\log_a y$.

$$y = a^x \iff x = \log_a y$$

2 Use this definition to find

(a) $\log_3 9$ (b) $\log_5 125$ (c) $\log_5 \frac{1}{25}$ (d) $\log_7 1$ (e) $\log_6 \frac{1}{216}$

(f) $\log_3 \sqrt[4]{3}$ (g) $\log_4 2$ (h) $\log_{11} 11$ (i) $\log_3 -3$

3 What is (a) $\log_a 1$ (b) $\log_a a$ (c) $\log_a \dfrac{1}{a}$ (d) $\log_a a^2$?

4 Use your calculator to find (a) $\log_{10} 10^{3.7}$, (b) $10^{\log_{10} 3.7}$. Explain your findings.

5 (a) Write down (i) $\log_2 8$ (ii) $\log_2 16$ (iii) $\log_2 128$

(b) Since $8 \times 16 = 128$, you can write this as $2^a \times 2^b = 2^c$. What are a, b and c? How is c related to a and b?

(c) Use this to explain why $\log_2 8 + \log_2 16 = \log_2 (8 \times 16)$.

6 $3^2 \times 3^3 = 3^5$

Explain how this verifies that $\log_3 9 + \log_3 27 = \log_3 (9 \times 27)$.

7 (a) Use your calculator to verify that $3 \approx 10^{0.4771}$, $5 \approx 10^{0.6990}$.

(b) What is (i) $\log_{10} 3$ (ii) $\log_{10} 5$?

(c) Use these results to find $\log_{10} 15$.

8 Use your calculator to verify that $\log_{10} 9 + \log_{10} 8 = \log_{10} 72$.

Questions 5–8 suggest that logs are related by the law:

$$\log_a m + \log_a n = \log_a mn$$

In fact, it is possible to prove that this result is true for any positive base a by using the result

$$a^{\log_a x} = x$$

$$a^{\log_a m + \log_a n} = a^{\log_a m} \times a^{\log_a n} \quad \text{(law of indices)}$$
$$= m \times n$$
$$= a^{\log_a (mn)}$$
$$\Rightarrow \log_a m + \log_a n = \log_a (mn)$$

Question 9 extends this result to logs of quotients.

9 In the law above, replace n by $\dfrac{l}{m}$. Hence show that

$$\log_a l - \log_a m = \log_a \frac{l}{m}$$

Verify that this holds by choosing two arbitrary numbers for l and m.

10 $\log_{10} 2 = 0.3010 \qquad \log_{10} 3 = 0.4771$

Use the properties of logs and the result that $\log_{10} 10 = 1$ to find (in any order)

$\log_{10} \frac{1}{2},\quad \log_{10} 1.5,\quad \log_{10} 2.5,\quad \log_{10} 4,\quad \log_{10} 5,\quad \log_{10} 6,\quad \log_{10} 8,\quad \log_{10} 9$

$a^x = b$

1 (a) Use your calculator to find the relationship between

   (i) $\log_{10} 49$ and $\log_{10} 7$ (ii) $\log_{10} 64$ and $\log_{10} 2$ (iii) $\log_{10} 125$ and $\log_{10} 5$

   (b) What is the relationship between $\log_{10} m^p$ and $\log_{10} m$?

2 (a) Use the result $\log_a mn = \log_a m + \log_a n$ to explain why $\log_a m^2 = 2 \log_a m$.

   (b) Generalise this method to explain the law that you found in question 1(b).

3 What is the relationship between $\log 2^x$ and $\log 2$? By taking logs of both sides, use this relationship to solve the equation

   $$2^x = 7$$

4 £1000 is invested in an account which earns 1% interest per month, all interest being reinvested.

   (a) Explain why the number m of months taken for the total investment to reach £2000 is given by the equation

   $$1.01^m = 2$$

   (b) Find m.

5 The half-life, t days, of bismuth–210 is given approximately by the equation

   $$10 \times (0.87)^t = 5$$

Find its half-life in days, correct to 2 significant figures.

4 Radians

4.1 Rates of change

The two pictures show a boat moored to a post. One picture shows the situation about midway between low and high tide; the other is near to high tide.

The graph below is the one used previously to show the height of the tide.

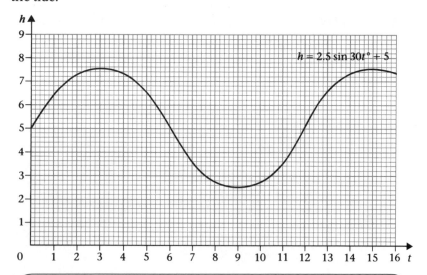

$$h = 2.5 \sin 30t° + 5$$

(a) At what times does the tide rise most rapidly?

(b) At what times does the tide fall most rapidly?

(c) When is the rate of change zero?

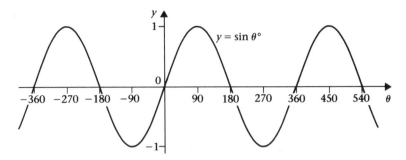

The graph of $y = \sin \theta°$ has gradient $\dfrac{dy}{d\theta}$.

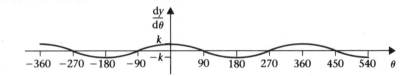

(a) Explain why the gradient graph is as shown.

(b) What can you say about the value of k?

(c) Note that the scales on the y- and θ-axes are very different. Roughly how large is k?

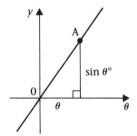

Zooming in to the origin on the graph of $y = \sin \theta°$ and using the principle of local straightness, the gradient of $y = \sin \theta°$ at the origin is

$$\frac{dy}{d\theta} \approx \frac{\sin \theta°}{\theta}$$

(a) What is the equation of the gradient graph?

(b) What is the connection between k and $\dfrac{\sin \theta°}{\theta}$?

(c) How can you obtain a good estimate of k?

TASKSHEET 1 — Differentiation of sin θ° (page 87)

The tasksheet demonstrates the result

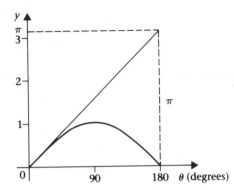

$$\frac{d}{d\theta}(\sin \theta)° = \frac{\pi}{180} \cos \theta°$$

At $(0, 0)$,

$$\text{gradient} = \frac{\pi}{180}$$

If angles were measured in units other than degrees, with π of these new units equivalent to $180°$, then the diagram above would look like this:

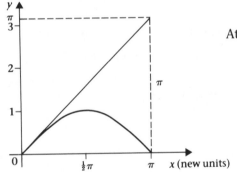

At $(0, 0)$,

$$\text{gradient} = \frac{\pi}{\pi} = 1$$

The new units would then give the simple result:

$$y = \sin x \implies \frac{dy}{dx} = \cos x$$

Scientific calculators provide the option of using these new units, which are called **radians** and are defined by the relationship

π radians $= 180°$

(a) Sketch the gradient graph for $y = \cos x°$.

(b) What do you think is the derivative of:

(i) $\cos x°$, (ii) $\cos x$ (x in radians)?

4.2 Radian measure

In most of the subsequent work on circular functions you will be using radians. It is often convenient to express radians as multiples of π, because the key relationship between radians and degrees is

π radians $= 180°$

The symbol for a radian is 1^c ('c' suggests *circular* measure); thus $\pi^c = 180°$. Except when the radian unit is being stressed, the c is usually omitted.

TASKSHEET 2 — Radian measure (page 88)

The following exercise may be attempted orally.

EXERCISE 1

1 Express these angles, measured in degrees, in radians.

(a) 90°   (b) 360°   (c) 45°   (d) 120°

(e) 60°   (f) 720°   (g) −30°   (h) 135°

2 Express these angles, measured in radians, in degrees.

(a) $\frac{1}{4}\pi$ (b) 3π (c) $-\pi$

(d) $\frac{3}{2}\pi$ (e) -2π

3 If the period of $y = \cos\theta°$ is 360, what is the period of $y = \cos\theta^c$?

4 What are the periods of the functions with these equations?

(a) $y = \sin t$ (b) $y = \sin\pi t$ (c) $y = \sin\omega t$

4.3 Area and arc lengths

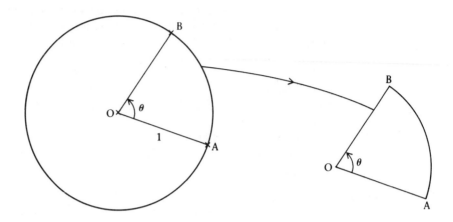

(a) What is the length of arc AB?

(b) What angle θ gives an arc length of 1 unit?

(c) Suggest a value for the area of sector AOB.

Radian measure for angles can be directly related to circles, and is therefore often called circular measure.

A radian is the angle subtended by an arc of unit length at the centre of a circle of unit radius.

For a sector of a circle radius r, with angle θ radians,

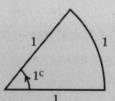

arc length $l = r\theta$

area $A = \frac{1}{2}r^2\theta$

EXERCISE 2

1   The wedge OAB is cut from a circle of radius 2 cm.

   (a) What is the area of the wedge?

   (b) What is the length of arc AB?

   (c) What is the perimeter of the wedge?

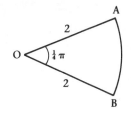

2

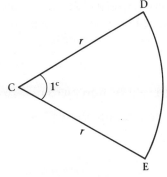

If the perimeter of sector CDE is numerically equal to the area of sector CDE, find *r*.

3   An area is to be fenced off for a crowd at a pop concert.

   (a) Calculate the length required to fence off the perimeter.

   (b) Calculate the maximum crowd if the police decide that the crowd density should not exceed 1 person per 2 square metres.

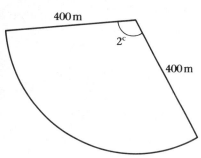

4   OAB is a sector of a circle of radius *r*. Find in terms of *r* and θ:

   (a) the length BC

   (b) the area of triangle OAB

   (c) the area of the sector OAB

   (d) the area of the shaded segment

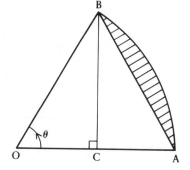

4.4 More about derivatives

You have seen that, when x is measured in radians,

$$y = \sin x \implies \frac{dy}{dx} = \cos x \qquad y = \cos x \implies \frac{dy}{dx} = -\sin x$$

You can use these results to find derivatives of functions such as sin $2x$, 5 cos x and 10 sin $0.1\,\pi x$. The graphs of such functions are related to those of sin x and cos x by means of stretches in the x- and y-directions. You have seen that a stretch of factor $\frac{1}{b}$ in the x-direction and a stretch of a in the y-direction maps $y = \sin x$ onto $y = a \sin bx$.

In the next tasksheet you can use these ideas to find the derivative of $y = a \sin bx$.

TASKSHEET 3 — Further derivatives (page 90)

You have now seen that:

> With x in radians,
> $$y = a \sin bx \implies \frac{dy}{dx} = a\,b \cos bx$$
> $$y = a \cos bx \implies \frac{dy}{dx} = -a\,b \sin bx$$

EXERCISE 3

1 Find $\dfrac{dy}{dx}$ when

(a) $y = \frac{1}{2}\sin x$ (b) $y = 5 \cos x$ (c) $y = 0.1 \sin x + 0.5$

(d) $y = \sin 4x$ (e) $y = \cos 2\pi x$ (f) $y = \sin 0.2x$

(g) $y = 3 \cos 2x$ (h) $y = 6 \sin \frac{1}{2}\pi x$ (i) $y = 4 + 3 \sin \frac{1}{3}x$

2 (a) If $y = \cos 2x$, what is $\dfrac{dy}{dx}$?   (b) Find $\displaystyle\int \sin 2x\,dx$.   (c) Find $\displaystyle\int \cos 3x\,dx$.

TASKSHEET 4E — Derivative of sin² x (page 91)

4.5 Applications

Returning to the example involving the height of the tide, you can reformulate it in terms of radians so that it is easier to answer questions about rates of change.

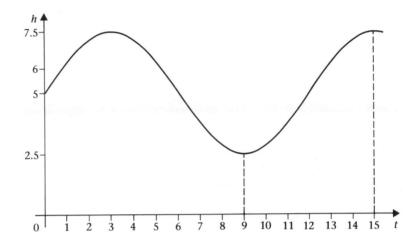

(a) What is the period of the function which describes the height of the tide?

(b) If the height of the tide is h metres at time t hours, then explain why $h = 2.5 \sin \frac{1}{6}\pi t + 5$

Differentiating to find the rate at which the tide is changing at any time,

$$\frac{dh}{dt} = \frac{5}{12}\pi \cos \frac{1}{6}\pi t$$

Why $\dfrac{5}{12}\pi$?

When $t = 0$, $\dfrac{dh}{dt} = \dfrac{5}{12}\pi = 1.3$ (to 2 s.f.)

The tide is rising most rapidly when $t = 0$, (and also when $t = 12$, 24, . . .) and the rate of rise is 1.3 metres per hour. You can use the formula for $\dfrac{dh}{dt}$ to find the rate of change at any time.

(a) When $t = 4$, what is the value of $\dfrac{dh}{dt}$ to 2 s.f.?

(b) State what this means.

(c) At what other times will $\dfrac{dh}{dt}$ have this value?

EXERCISE 4

1 A mass oscillates up and down at the end of a spring. The length of the spring in centimetres after time t seconds is given by the equation

$$L = 12 + 2.5 \cos 2\pi t$$

(a) Find the derivative, $\dfrac{dL}{dt}$. Sketch the graphs of L and $\dfrac{dL}{dt}$ against t.

(b) Calculate, when $t = 0, 0.1, 0.25, 0.4$ and 0.5,

(i) the length of the spring, (ii) the velocity of the mass.

Comment on the results.

2 The height in metres of the tide at a harbour entrance is given by

$$h = 0.8 \cos \tfrac{1}{6}\pi t + 6.5$$

where t is the time in hours measured from high tide.

(a) Find the derivative, $\dfrac{dh}{dt}$. Sketch graphs of h and $\dfrac{dh}{dt}$ against t for a 24-hour interval.

(b) Calculate the two times during the first 12 hours when the height of the tide is 6 metres. Find the rate of change of height at both these times and comment on the results.

(c) When is the tide falling most rapidly during the first 12 hours? Find the rate at which it is then falling.

(d) When is the speed of the tidal current least and when is it greatest? What factors are important in deciding when it is safe to enter or leave the harbour?

3 The height in metres above ground level of a chair on a big wheel is given by

$$h = 5.6 - 4.8 \cos \tfrac{1}{30}\pi t$$

where t is the time measured in seconds.

(a) Find the derivative, $\dfrac{dh}{dt}$, and sketch graphs of h and $\dfrac{dh}{dt}$ against t for a two-minute interval.

(b) Between what times is the chair descending at a rate greater than 0.4 metre per second? When is the chair descending most rapidly and at what speed?

4 (a) The heights of the tide at Sheerness on a certain September day were 4.6 m at high water and 1.7 m at low water.

 (i) Assuming a period of 12 hours and measuring the time in hours from high tide, sketch a graph of the height from 6 hours before to 6 hours after high water.

 (ii) Suggest a suitable formula for h, the height in metres, in terms of t, the time in hours.

(b) The currents in the Thames estuary near to Sheerness are given in the following table.

Hours before high water	5	4	3	2	1
Current in knots	0.7	0.9	1.1	1.0	0.7

 (i) Assuming that the currents after high water are the same, but in the opposite direction, sketch the graph of current against time from 6 hours before to 6 hours after high water.

 (ii) Suggest a suitable formula for the current in knots in terms of the time in hours.

 (iii) How is this related to the height equation found in part (a)?

85

(c) (i) Find the rate of change of h and sketch a graph of $\dfrac{dh}{dt}$ against t for the same values as those in the previous graphs.

(ii) Comment on the relationship between this and the graph of the current.

After working through this chapter you should:

1 be able to understand and use radian measure;

2 know that the period of $y = \sin \omega t$ is $\dfrac{2\pi}{\omega}$;

3 know that for a sector of angle θ radius r,

$$\text{arc length} = r\theta$$

$$\text{area} = \frac{1}{2}r^2\theta$$

4 be able to differentiate circular functions and know that, for x in radians,

$$\frac{d}{dx}(a \sin bx) = a\,b \cos bx$$

$$\frac{d}{dx}(a \cos bx) = -a\,b \sin bx$$

Differentiation of sin $\theta°$

1

You will need a graph plotter which can plot the gradient graph of a function.

1 (a) (i) Calculate the values of $\dfrac{\sin \theta°}{\theta}$ for $\theta = 10, 5, 2, 1$ and 0.1.

(ii) To what value does your sequence of values of $\dfrac{\sin \theta°}{\theta}$ converge, as θ approaches zero?

(b) Use a graph plotter to obtain the gradient graph of $y = \sin \theta°$. Does this give a value of k which agrees with your solution to part (a)? You will need to be careful with the vertical scale.

2

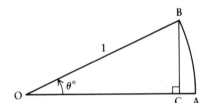

Consider a sector AOB of a circle of unit radius with angle $\theta°$ at the centre. BC is the perpendicular from B to OA.

(a) For $\theta = 10, 5, 2, 1$ and 0.1 calculate:

(i) the length of BC, (ii) the length of the arc BA.

(b) What do you notice about the results?

3 Express the length BC and the length of arc BA as functions of θ.

From the previous question it is evident that these two lengths are approximately equal for small values of θ. Use this fact to explain why

$$\frac{\sin \theta°}{\theta} \approx \frac{\pi}{180}$$

for small values of θ.

4 Calculate the value of $\dfrac{\pi}{180}$ and compare it with the answer to question 1.

5 What is the gradient of $y = \sin \theta°$ at the origin?

6 Suggest a suitable expression for $\dfrac{dy}{d\theta}$, if $y = \sin \theta°$.

Radian measure

You will need a radian measurer.

1   Using the result π radians = 180°, calculate:

   (a) 1 radian in degrees (to three decimal places);

   (b) 1 degree in radians (to five decimal places).

2   Use the radian measurer to measure the following angles in radians, quoting your answer in terms of multiples of π where appropriate.

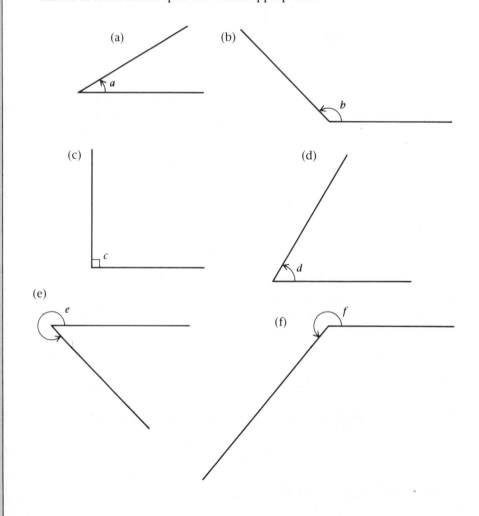

3 Try to draw the following angles and use the radian measurer to check your estimate.

(a) 0.5 radians   (b) 2 radians   (c) 0.3 radians

Calculators will accept either degrees or radians as input for circular functions. The following examples allow you to explore the different modes on your calculator.

4 Use your calculator in appropriate mode to find

(a) $\sin 1^c$ (b) $\sin 1°$ (c) $\cos -5°$ (d) $\cos -5^c$

(e) $\tan \frac{1}{4}\pi^c$ (f) $\tan \frac{1}{4}\pi°$

5 (a) Find   (i) $\sin 30°$,   (ii) $\sin \frac{1}{6}\pi^c$.   What do you notice?

(b) You know π radians are equal to $180°$. This can be used to establish a number of other reference points between the two scales. Complete the following table.

Radians		$\frac{1}{2}\pi$			$\frac{1}{6}\pi$	$\frac{3}{2}\pi$	
Degrees	180		60	45			360

(c) What formula will convert $\theta°$ to radians?

(d) What formula will convert θ^c to degrees?

6 It is very easy to leave your calculator in the wrong mode! Suppose you are asked to find $\sin \frac{1}{3}\pi$ and you have your machine in degree mode.

(a) What is $\frac{1}{3}\pi$ to 3 decimal places?

(b) What is $\sin \frac{1}{3}\pi$ (taking $\frac{1}{3}\pi$ in radians)?

(c) What answer does your calculator give if left in degree mode?

7 Suppose you try to evaluate $\sin 60°$, but leave your calculator in radian mode. What should you get in degree mode? What in fact do you get?

8 Working in radians, plot on graph paper the graph of $y = \sin x$ for values of x from 0 to 7, increasing in steps of 0.5. In addition, mark on the x-axis the numbers $\frac{1}{4}\pi$, $\frac{1}{2}\pi$, $\frac{3}{4}\pi$, π, $\frac{3}{2}\pi$, 2π.

Further derivatives

It is important to remember that x is measured in **radians** throughout. You will need a graph plotter which can plot the gradient graph of a function.

1   On the same axes sketch the graphs of $y = \sin x$ and $y = 5 \sin x$ for $0 \leq x \leq 2\pi$.

(a) Describe the stretch which maps $y = \sin x$ onto $y = 5 \sin x$.

(b) What is the effect of this stretch on the gradient of the graph of $y = \sin x$?

(c) Suggest what the derivative of $y = 5 \sin x$ might be.

(d) Check your answer to (c) by using a graph plotter to obtain the gradient graph for $y = 5 \sin x$.

2   On the same axes, sketch the graphs of $y = \sin x$ and $y = \sin 3x$ for $0 \leq x \leq 2\pi$.

(a) Describe the stretch which maps $y = \sin x$ onto $y = \sin 3x$.

(b) What is the effect of this stretch on the gradient of the graph of $y = \sin x$?

(c) Suggest what the derivative of $y = \sin 3x$ might be. Check your answer by using a graph plotter.

3   Investigate the derivative of $y = 5 \sin 3x$ in a similar way.

4   Using the ideas of the previous questions, find the derivatives of:

(a) $y = \cos 2x$ (b) $y = 10 \sin 2x$ (c) $y = \sin 0.5x$

5   (a) Sketch graphs of $y = 3 \cos 2x$, $y = 3 \cos 2x + 4$ and $y = 3 \cos 2x - 1$.

(b) What are the derivatives of each of these functions?

6   What are the derivatives of:

(i) $y = a \sin x$ (ii) $y = \sin bx$ (iii) $y = a \sin bx$?

(b) Write down the corresponding results for cosine functions.

Derivative of sin²x

1 (a) Sketch the graph of $y = \sin^2 x$.

   (b) By sketching the gradient graph of $y = \sin^2 x$, suggest an appropriate expression for the derivative of $\sin^2 x$.

2 (a) $\sin^2 x$ may be written as $a \cos bx + c$. What are the values of a, b, c?

   (b) Use your results in (a) to write down the derivative of $\sin^2 x$. Compare your answer with that found in question 1.

3 Find the derivative of $\cos^2 x$, checking your answer.

4 (a) Find the derivative of $\sin^2 x + \cos^2 x$.

   (b) Sketch the graph of $y = \sin^2 x + \cos^2 x$.

   (c) Explain the result in (a), using your graph.

5 e

5.1 e^x

You have seen in chapter 3 how functions given by equations of the form $y = Ka^x$ can be used to model growth. In this chapter you are going to look in detail at **rates** of growth for these functions and see how all functions of this kind are very closely related.

The number of bacteria in a colony increases exponentially with a growth factor of 2 per hour. From the time when there are 1000 bacteria it will therefore take one hour for the number to increase by 1000.

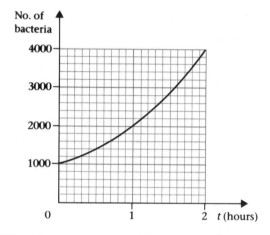

(a) Is the rate at which the colony is growing when it contains 1000 bacteria less than, equal to or greater than 1000 per hour?

(b) When the population is 2000, is the rate of growth less than, equal to or greater than 2000 per hour?

(c) What is meant by the rate of growth and how can you calculate it?

(d) Will the rate of growth and the size of the population always be related as in parts (a) and (b)?

TASKSHEET   1 or 1E   –   Rates of growth (page 101 or 102)

The gradient of an exponential function at any point is proportional to its value at that point.

$$y = 2^x \quad \Rightarrow \quad \frac{dy}{dx} = 0.69 \times 2^x$$

$$y = 3^x \quad \Rightarrow \quad \frac{dy}{dx} = 1.10 \times 3^x$$

$$y = 10^x \quad \Rightarrow \quad \frac{dy}{dx} = 2.30 \times 10^x$$

Generally $y = a^x \quad \Rightarrow \quad \frac{dy}{dx} = k \times a^x$, where k is a constant.

The value of a for which $k = 1$ is denoted by the letter e. This gives the important result

$$\frac{d}{dx}(e^x) = e^x$$

What is $\int e^x \, dx$?

e = 2.718 281 828 4 to ten decimal places.

Like π, e is an irrational number. The Swiss mathematician Leonhard Euler (1707–1783) first used the letter e to represent this number. Euler introduced several other mathematical notations, including that for functions, f(x). He was also the first to use the summation sign $\sum$, the letter π for the ratio of circumference to diameter of a circle and i for $\sqrt{-1}$. He continued to work actively after becoming totally blind in 1768.

93

The shapes of the graphs of $y = e^x$ and $y = e^{-x}$ are typical of exponential growth and decay respectively.

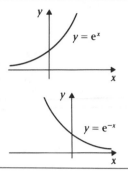

Some calculators and textbooks express e^x as exp x. This notation is also used in some computer languages.

EXERCISE 1

1   (a) Use your calculator to find

(i) e^3 (ii) exp (5.1)   (iii) e^{-2} (iv) $\dfrac{5}{e^3}$ (v) exp (0.5)

(b) What is the largest power of e that your calculator can evaluate, and why?

2   Make tables of values for $-4 \leq x \leq 4$ and draw the graphs of

(a) $y = e^{2x}$ (b) $y = e^{-x}$

3   Draw the graph of

$$y = 5(1 - e^{-x})$$

for $0 \leq x \leq 5$. Check the shape using a graph plotter.

4   (a) When certain drugs are injected into the body, the amount remaining in the bloodstream decays exponentially. The amount of one drug in the bloodstream is modelled by the equation

$$y = 5e^{-0.2t}$$

where t is the time in hours after the dose is administered, and y is the amount remaining, in milligrams.

(i) What is the initial value of y?

(ii) What is the value of y when $t = 10$?

(iii) Sketch the graph of y against t.

(b) The amount of a second drug is modelled by the equation $y = 5e^{-0.5t}$. Does it decay more or less rapidly than the first drug?

5   A colony of bacteria grows according to the law $y = 4e^t$, where t is measured in hours and y is the population.

By differentiating, show that $\dfrac{dy}{dt} = y$. What does this tell you about the rate of growth of the bacterial colony?

How rapidly is the colony growing at a time when it contains 500 bacteria?

5.2 e^{ax}

One of the great benefits of introducing e as a base for the growth function is that it can replace all the other bases. This simplifies subsequent work, particularly in calculus.

(a) How are 2^{2t} and 4^t related? Why?

(b) Can you find alternative expressions of the form 2^{at} to represent   (i) 8^t,   (ii) 5^t?

(c) Is it **always** possible to express b^t in the form 2^{at}?

TASKSHEET 2 – e^{ax} (page 103)

Tasksheet 2 has shown that if $b > 0$ you can express b^x in the form e^{ax} and that

$$\frac{d}{dx}(e^{ax}) = ae^{ax}$$

(a) What is $\int e^{ax}\, dx$?

(b) In general, if $\dfrac{d}{dx}(f(x)) = g(x)$, what are

   (i) $\dfrac{d}{dx}(f(ax))$ (ii) $\int g(ax)\, dx$?

E X A M P L E   1

Find the derivatives of (a) $3e^{5x}$, (b) $\dfrac{1}{e^{2x}}$.

S O L U T I O N

(a) $\dfrac{d}{dx}(3e^{5x}) = 3 \times 5e^{5x} = 15e^{5x}$

(b) $\dfrac{d}{dx}\left(\dfrac{1}{e^{2x}}\right) = \dfrac{d}{dx}(e^{-2x}) = -2e^{-2x} = \dfrac{-2}{e^{2x}}$

95

EXERCISE 2

1 Differentiate:

   (a) e^{4x} (b) e^{-2x} (c) $(e^x)^5$ (d) $\dfrac{1}{e^{3x}}$

   (e) $5e^{4x}$ (f) $e^x + \dfrac{1}{e^x}$ (g) $\sqrt{e^x}$ (h) $\dfrac{5}{e^{9x}}$

2 Integrate the functions of x in question 1.

3 Sketch the graphs of:

   (a) $y = e^{-4x}$ (b) $y = 3(1 - e^{-2x})$ for $x \geq 0$ (c) $y = e^x + \dfrac{1}{e^x}$

4 When a drug such a penicillin is prescribed, it is usual to take it 3 or 4 times a day. One or two days may elapse before the drug starts to take effect. A simple model of this process is known as the 'Rustogi' drug model.

   Suppose that for a certain drug, the amount in milligrams in the bloodstream t hours after taking a dose of size A mg is given by

   $$x = Ae^{-\frac{1}{8}t}$$

   and that a dose of 10 mg is administered at 8-hourly intervals. On graph paper, using a scale of 1 cm to 2 hours on the t-axis and 1 cm to 2 mg on the x-axis, plot the drug level in the body over the first 32 hours as follows:

   (a) For the first 8 hours calculate the drug level for $t = 0, 2, 4, 6, 8$ and plot these values.

   (b) Add the next dose of 10 mg and plot this point, also at $t = 8$.

   (c) This gives the 'effective dose' at this time i.e. the new value for A. Recalculate the drug level for the next 8-hour period, again taking $t = 0$, 2, 4, 6, 8.

   (d) Repeat steps (b) and (c) to show how the drug level varies in the body for the remainder of the period.

   What value does the maximum drug level in the body approach?

5 In hospitals, when it is necessary for a patient to respond rapidly to treatment, a doctor will often give a 'booster' dose, equivalent to 1.6 times the initial dose. Repeat question 4, but with an initial dose of 16 mg and subsequent doses of 10 mg. [It should only be necessary to consider the first 8 hours.]

   Note: this method is not used for drugs available on prescription to the general public; if subsequent doses of 16 mg were taken in error the drug level would rise to $1.6 \times 16 = 25.6$ mg, with potentially dangerous consequences.

5.3 The natural log

You saw in section 3.4 that the power of 2 that was equal to y was called $\log_2 y$, i.e.

if $2^x = y$, then $x = \log_2 y$

You also saw how this idea can be extended to other bases, so that, for example, if $10^x = y$ then $x = \log_{10} y$.

Since e was chosen as the base for exponential functions in order to simplify results in calculus, it is natural to consider e as a base for logarithms. Logarithms to base e are called **natural logarithms** and $\log_e x$ may be written as $\ln x$ (n for 'natural'). Some older texts simply use $\log x$ for $\ln x$.

> (a) How would you define $\ln x$?
>
> (b) Use your calculator to find· (i) $\ln e^{2.3}$ (ii) $e^{\ln 4.3}$
>
> Explain your results.

At this stage you may find it useful to recall the laws of logarithms, as applied to logarithms with base e.

$\ln e = 1 \qquad \ln 1 = 0$

$\ln(ab) = \ln a + \ln b \qquad \ln\left(\dfrac{a}{b}\right) = \ln a - \ln b$

$\ln(a^n) = n \ln a$

E X A M P L E 2

Express in terms of $\ln x$

(a) $\ln 4x^5$ (b) $\ln\left(\dfrac{1}{\sqrt{x}}\right)$

S O L U T I O N

(a) $\ln 4x^5 = \ln 4 + \ln x^5 = \ln 4 + 5 \ln x$

(b) $\ln\left(\dfrac{1}{\sqrt{x}}\right) = \ln 1 - \ln \sqrt{x} = 0 - \ln x^{\frac{1}{2}} = -\dfrac{1}{2} \ln x$

Natural logarithms are often called Napierian logarithms, after John Napier. However, this is a misnomer for they are not the logarithms originally developed by Napier.

  TASKSHEET 3 – Properties of ln x (page 105)

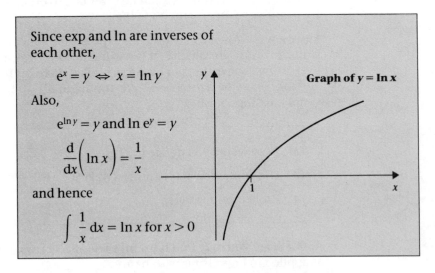

As you have seen, physical situations involving growth are often modelled using exponential functions. In solving the model, a useful step is that from an equation of the form $e^A = B$ to one of the form $A = \ln B$. An example of this is in the use of the logistic curve, a model that is appropriate when growth is limited by fixed resources.

Its general equation is

$$y = \frac{A}{1 + Ke^{-\lambda x}}$$

where A, K and λ are constants, and its graph is as shown.

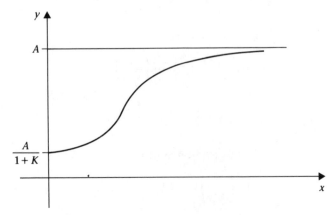

98

EXAMPLE 3

A highly infectious disease is introduced into a small isolated village, of population 200. The number of individuals y who have contracted the disease t days after the outbreak begins is modelled by the logistic equation.

$$y = \frac{200}{1 + 199e^{-0.2t}}$$

After what time has half the population been infected?

SOLUTION

When half the population has been infected $y = 100$.

$$100 = \frac{200}{1 + 199e^{-0.2t}}$$

$\Rightarrow \qquad 100\,(1 + 199e^{-0.2t}) = 200$

$\Rightarrow \qquad 1 + 199e^{-0.2t} = 2$

$\Rightarrow \qquad e^{-0.2t} = \frac{1}{199}$

$\Rightarrow \qquad -0.2t = \ln \frac{1}{199}$

$\Rightarrow \qquad t = -\frac{1}{0\cdot2} \ln \frac{1}{199} = 26.5 \text{ (days)}$

EXERCISE 3

1 Use your calculator to evaluate

(a) $\ln 3.5$ (b) $\ln 0.35$ (c) $\ln 7$

2 (a) Use your calculator to verify

(i) $\ln 3 + \ln 4 = \ln 12$ (ii) $\ln 10 - \ln 2 = \ln 5$

(iii) $3 \ln 5 = \ln 125$ (iv) $\dfrac{\ln 20}{\ln 4} \neq \ln 5$

(b) Use the laws of logarithms to explain the results in (a).

3 Use the laws of logarithms to express the following in terms of $\ln x$.

(a) $\ln x^3$ (b) $\ln 4x$ (c) $\ln \frac{1}{3}x$

4 Find   (a) $\dfrac{d}{dx}(4 \ln x)$ (b) $\dfrac{d}{dx}(\ln x^3)$ (c) $\dfrac{d}{dx}(\ln 4x)$

5 Use the population model of example 3 to find how long it takes for 90% of the population to become infected.

6 A cup of coffee, initially at boiling point, cools according to Newton's law of cooling, so that after t minutes its temperature $T°C$ is given by

$$T = 15 + 85\,e^{-t/8}$$

Sketch the graph of T against t.

How long does it take for the cup to cool to $40°C$?

7 In the process of carbon dating, the level of the isotope carbon-14 (C_{14}) is measured. When a plant or animal is alive the amount of C_{14} in the body remains at a constant level, but when it dies the amount decays at a constant rate according to the law $m = m_0 e^{-Kt}$, where m_0 is the initial mass and m the mass after t years.

(a) If the half-life of C_{14} is 5570 years, find the decay constant K.

(b) A piece of oak from an old building contains $\frac{9}{10}$ of the level of C_{14} that is contained in living oak. How old is the building?

After working through this chapter you should:

1 understand the reason for the choice of e as base for exponential and logarithmic functions;

2 be able to sketch graphs of exponential growth and decay and of logarithmic functions;

3 be able to differentiate e^{ax} and $\ln ax$, and to integrate e^{ax} and $\frac{1}{x}$;

4 appreciate that exp and ln are inverse functions;

5 be able to solve problems involving e^x and $\ln x$ by using appropriate algebraic manipulation.

Rates of growth

You will need a graph plotter which can plot the gradient graph of a function.

1 (a) Sketch on the same axes the graphs of $y = 2^x$ and $\dfrac{dy}{dx}$, the gradient function.

   (b) Suggest an equation for the function $\dfrac{dy}{dx}$, and check your answer using a graph plotter.

2 Repeat question 1 for each of the following functions:

   (a) $y = 3^x$ (b) $y = 1.5^x$ (c) $y = 10^x$

3 (a) Complete the following table:

a	$\dfrac{d}{dx}(a^x)$
1.5	
2	
3	
10	

   NB. The notation $\dfrac{d}{dx}(\ \ )$ is used as a shorthand. For example, you could write

   $\dfrac{d}{dx}(x^2) = 2x$ instead of 'if $y = x^2$, then $\dfrac{dy}{dx} = 2x$'.

   (b) Use your table to suggest a value for a for which

   $$\frac{d}{dx}(a^x) = a^x$$

   Check your answer by sketching appropriate graphs.

4 (a) If e is the value of a you found in question 3(b), how is the graph of $y = 2e^x$ related to the graph of e^x?

   (b) Use this result to write down the gradient function for $2e^x$.

   (c) Suggest an appropriate gradient function for ke^x.

Rates of growth

You will need a graph plotter which can plot the gradient graph of a function.

1 (a) Sketch the graphs of $y = 2^x$ and $\dfrac{dy}{dx}$, the gradient function.

  (b) Suggest an equation for the function $\dfrac{dy}{dx}$, and check your answer using a graph plotter.

2 Repeat question 1 for each of the following functions:

  (a) $y = 3^x$ (b) $y = 1.5^x$ (c) $y = 10^x$

3 Suggest a value for a for which $\dfrac{d}{dx}(a^x) = a^x$. Check your answer by sketching appropriate graphs.

4 Suggest an appropriate gradient function for ke^x, where e is the value for a that you found in question 3.

The gradient function for $y = 2^x$ can be found by 'zooming-in' at any point P (x, y) on the graph of $y = 2^x$ until the curve looks straight.

The gradient of the graph at P is approximately equal to the gradient of PQ, where Q is a nearby point on the graph.

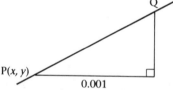

5 (a) Explain why the y-coordinate of Q is $2^{0.001}\, 2^x$.

  (b) Explain why the gradient of PQ is $\dfrac{2^{0.001}\, 2^x - 2^x}{0.001}$.

  (c) Show how the expression in (b) can be simplified to 0.693×2^x.

  (c) You have seen that $y = 2^x \Rightarrow \dfrac{dy}{dx} \approx 0.693 \times 2^x$. How could you increase the accuracy of this result?

6 Adapt the method of question 5 to find $\dfrac{dy}{dx}$ when $y = 5^x$.

7 Given that e is the value you found in question 3, explain why $\dfrac{e^{0.001} - 1}{0.001} \approx 1$.

e ^{ax} *TASKSHEET* **2**

1   (a) Use a graph plotter to verify that the graphs of 9^x and 3^{2x} coincide.

    (b) Find the value of a so that the following pairs of graphs coincide.

      (i) 5^x and 3^{ax} (ii) 7^x and 3^{ax} (iii) 2^x and 3^{ax}

It appears that, for any positive value of b, you could replace b^x by 3^{ax}. In other words, only one base is needed for all exponential functions. The base used in practice is not 3 but e.

2   (a) Use a graph plotter to sketch the family of curves $y = e^{ax}$

      (i) for a few positive values of a, of your own choice,

      (ii) for a few negative values of a.

      What shape is the graph if $a = 0$?

    (b) If $a > b > 0$, describe the relationship of the graph of e^{ax} to that of e^{bx}. For what values of x is $e^{ax} > e^{bx}$?

3   Using the same method as in question 1, find the value of a so that the following pairs of graphs coincide.

    (a) 5^x and e^{ax} (b) 8^x and e^{ax} (c) 2^x and e^{ax}

4   (a) You know from section 5.1 that, if $y = 2^x$, $\dfrac{dy}{dx} \approx 0.69 \times 2^x$ and, from question 3, that $2^x \approx e^{0.69x}$. Explain how these results can be combined to show that

$$\frac{d}{dx}\left(e^{0.69x}\right) = 0.69\,e^{0.69x}$$

    (b) Suggest a possible derivative for e^{5x}.

103

The previous question suggests that $\dfrac{d}{dx}\,(e^{ax}) = ae^{ax}$. In the next question you can investigate how this result arises.

5

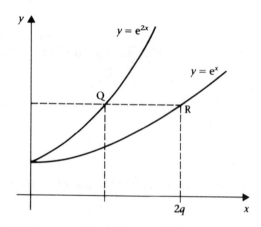

(a) In the diagram, Q and R have the same y-coordinate. What is it?

(b) What is the x-coordinate of Q?

(c) The graph of $y = e^{2x}$ can be obtained from the graph of $y = e^x$ by squashing by a factor of 2 in the x-direction. What effect does this have on the gradient of the graph?

(d) If the gradient at R is g, what is the gradient at Q?

(e) Write down, in terms of q the gradient of $y = e^x$ at the point R. Hence write down the gradient of $y = e^{2x}$ at the point Q.

(f) Complete:

$$\frac{d}{dx}\,(e^{2x}) = \ldots\ldots\ldots \times e^{2x}$$

Properties of ln *x*

The graph of ln *x*

1 (a) ln y (= $\log_e y$) is the power of e that equals y, i.e. $y = e^x \Leftrightarrow x = \ln y$. Use this result to find

   (i) ln 1   (ii) ln e   (iii) ln e^2

   (iv) ln $\dfrac{1}{e}$ (v) ln $\dfrac{1}{e^5}$ (vi) ln(−1)

   (b) Use your results to sketch the graph of ln x.

2 Plot the graphs of $y = \ln x$ and $y = e^x$ on the same axes, ensuring that x and y scales are identical. Explain the relationship between the two.

Derivative

3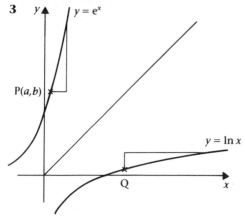

The figure shows the graphs of $y = e^x$ and $y = \ln x$. Q is the reflection of P (a, b) in the line $y = x$.

You can use the relationship between the two graphs to find the gradient of $y = \ln x$ at Q.

   (a) Express b in terms of a.

   (b) Write down the coordinates of Q.

   (c) Use the fact that the triangle at Q is a reflection of the triangle at P to explain why the gradient of the curve at Q is $\dfrac{1}{\text{gradient of } y = e^x \text{ at P}}$.

   (d) Since P lies on the curve $y = e^x$, you know that the gradient at P (a, b) is e^a. What is the gradient of $y = \ln x$ at Q?

   (e) Explain why $\dfrac{d}{dx} (\ln x) = \dfrac{1}{x}$.

6 Transformations

6.1 Graph sketching

You will have noticed that the transformations of graphs have formed a central theme throughout the unit. You have seen several examples where a simple algebraic transformation of the equation of a function has brought about a geometric transformation of the graph.

 TASKSHEET 1 — Transforming equations (page 111)

Algebraic transformation of the equation	Geometric transformation of the graph
Replace x with kx	One-way sketch from the y-axis, scale factor $\dfrac{1}{k}$
Replace y with ky	One-way sketch from the x-axis, scale factor $\dfrac{1}{k}$
Replace x with $x + k$	Translation $\begin{bmatrix} -k \\ 0 \end{bmatrix}$
Replace y with $y + k$	Translation $\begin{bmatrix} 0 \\ -k \end{bmatrix}$
Replace x with $-x$	Reflection in the y-axis
Replace y with $-y$	Reflection in the x-axis
Interchange x and y	Reflection in $y = x$

Combining transformations can produce interesting effects. Suppose the equation $y = x^2 - 6x + 11$ has the algebraic transformation 'x is replaced with $-x$' followed by 'y is replaced with $-y$' applied to it. The new equation is

$$(-y) = (-x)^2 - 6(-x) + 11$$
$$\Rightarrow \quad -y = x^2 + 6x + 11$$
$$\Rightarrow \quad y = -x^2 - 6x - 11$$

Use a graph plotter to sketch the equation before and after the transformations.

What single geometric transformation is produced by replacing x with $-x$ and y with $-y$?

Understanding the relationship between algebraic and geometric transformations can help you sketch the graphs of quite complicated functions.

EXAMPLE 1

Describe the transformations which map the graph of $y = e^x$ onto $y = 2e^{3x + 1}$

SOLUTION

Replace x with $x + 1$

Translate $\begin{bmatrix} -1 \\ 0 \end{bmatrix}$

Replace x with $3x$.
One-way stretch from the y-axis, scale factor $\frac{1}{3}$.

Replace y with $\frac{1}{2}y$
One-way stretch from the x-axis, scale factor 2.

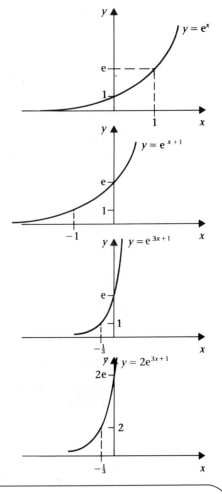

In the example above, what would happen if you replaced x with $3x$ **before** you replaced x with $x + 1$?

6.2 Stretching a circle

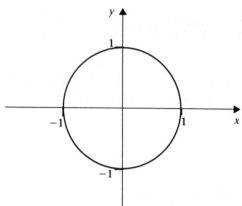

$x^2 + y^2 = 1$ is the equation of a circle, centre $(0, 0)$, radius 1.

Rearranging the equation gives $y = \pm \sqrt{(1 - x^2)}$, and plotting $y = \sqrt{(1 - x^2)}$ followed by $y = -\sqrt{(1 - x^2)}$ gives the graph of the full circle. Make sure that the same scale is used on both axes so that your graph will look like a circle.

> Is y a function of x?

Replacing x with $\frac{1}{3}x$ and y with $(y - 2)$ gives the equation

$$(\tfrac{1}{3}x)^2 + (y - 2)^2 = 1$$

> (a) Describe what effect replacing x with $\frac{1}{3}x$ and y with $(y - 2)$ has on the graph of $x^2 + y^2 = 1$.
>
> (b) Sketch the graph of $(\frac{1}{3}x)^2 + (y - 2)^2 = 1$.
>
> (c) Rearrange the equation into the form $y = \ldots$ so that you can plot the graph.

(a) What is the equation of a circle, radius r, centre $(0, 0)$?

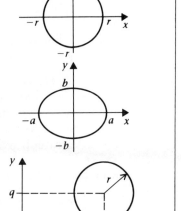

(b) What is the equation of the ellipse shown in the diagram?

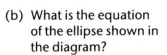

(c) What is the equation of a circle, radius r, centre (p, q)?

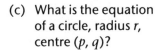

The shape of an ellipse is defined by the lengths of its major and minor axes. You can obtain the shape of an ellipse by stretching a unit circle along the x- and y-axes. You can then translate the shape to any location on the grid.

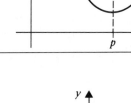

EXAMPLE 2

Give the equation of the ellipse shown in the diagram.

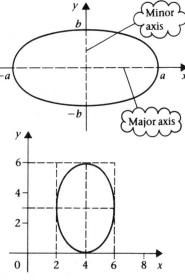

SOLUTION

The unit circle, $x^2 + y^2 = 1$, can be transformed onto the ellipse by a one-way stretch factor 2 along the x-axis and a one-way stretch factor 3 along the y-axis (replace x with $\frac{1}{2}x$ and y with $\frac{1}{3}y$) giving

$$(\tfrac{1}{2}x)^2 + (\tfrac{1}{3}y)^2 = 1$$

This is followed by a translation $\begin{bmatrix} 4 \\ 3 \end{bmatrix}$ (replace x with $x - 4$ and y with $y - 3$). The equation of the ellipse is $[\frac{1}{2}(x - 4)]^2 + [\frac{1}{3}(y - 3)]^2 = 1$

109

The technique of taking a basic graph and transforming it to fit another has been used several times throughout the unit. You have, for example, seen how both stretches and translations are used to fit the graph of $y = \sin x$ to the graph of $y = a \sin (bx + c) + d$. You will also recall that it was understanding the effect a stretch has on the gradient of a graph that enabled you to differentiate $y = a \sin x$, $y = \sin bx$ and $y = e^{ax}$.

You have also seen how transformations can be used to enhance your understanding of some functions. Understanding how two distinct transformations can be used to map the graph of $y = \ln x$ onto the graph of $y = \ln ax$ should, for example, have given you a greater insight into the log function.

EXERCISE 1

1   The graph of $y = \ln x$ can be fitted to the graph of $y = \ln 3x$ by either a one-way stretch or a translation. Describe the transformation in each case.

2   The graph of $y = x^2$ can be fitted to the graph of $y = 4x^2$ by either

      (a) a one-way stretch along the x-axis from $x = 0$

or   (b) a one-way stretch along the y-axis from $y = 0$

What is the stretch factor in each case?

3   The equation of the ellipse shown in the diagram can be obtained by transforming the unit circle. The unit circle can be fitted to the ellipse in two ways:

      (a) a stretch followed by a translation

      (b) a translation followed by a stretch

Specify the transformations in each case and hence obtain the equation of the ellipse in two different ways.

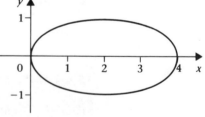

After working through this chapter you should:

1   have a clear understanding of how simple algebraic transformations on the equation of a graph bring about geometric transformations of the graph;

2   know how to apply these transformations to a variety of basic graphs, particularly the unit circle;

3   appreciate the central role transformations have played throughout this unit.

Transforming equations

If the equation $y = x^2 - 4x$ is transformed by replacing y with $3y$, the new equation is $3y = x^2 - 4x$ or $y = \frac{1}{3}x^2 - \frac{4}{3}x$. By plotting the graphs of $y = x^2 - 4x$ and $y = \frac{1}{3}x^2 - \frac{4}{3}x$ you can observe the geometric effect of this algebraic transformation.

1   Investigate what effect

(a) replacing x with $x + k$ or $x - k$;

(b) replacing y with $y + k$ or $y - k$;

(c) replacing x with kx or $\dfrac{x}{k}$;

(d) replacing y with ky or $\dfrac{y}{k}$;

has on the graph of

(i) $y = \frac{1}{2}x^2 - 4x$

(ii) $y = \sin x$

(iii) $y = e^x$

(iv) $x^2 + y^2 = 1$ (You may need to plot both $y = \sqrt{(1 - x^2)}$ and $y = -\sqrt{(1 - x^2)}$.)

Choose various values for k and describe what geometrical transformation of the graph is produced by each of the four algebraic transformations described above.

2   What is the geometrical transformation of a graph when

(a) x is replaced with $-x$;

(b) y is replaced with $-y$;

(c) x and y are interchanged?

Solutions

1 Algebra of functions

1.1 Composition of functions

Show that the function f given by

$f(t) = \frac{5}{9}(t - 32)$

converts a temperature of t degrees Fahrenheit to Celsius.

The difference between boiling point and freezing point is 180 degrees on the Fahrenheit scale and 100 degrees on the Celsius scale. Thus each degree on the Fahrenheit scale corresponds to $\frac{180}{100} = \frac{5}{9}$ degree on the Celsius scale. So subtract 32 to make the freezing point zero, then multiply by $\frac{5}{9}$.

What does fg(t) mean?

The function g is followed by the function f; that is, the output from g is used as input to f, so

$fg(t) = \frac{5}{9}(t + 273) - 32$

EXERCISE 1

1 (a) (i) $2x^3 + 3$ (ii) $(2x + 3)^3$

   (b) (i) $\frac{2}{x} + 1$ (ii) $\frac{1}{2x + 1}$

   (c) (i) $3(5 - x) + 2 = 17 - 3x$ (ii) $5 - (3x + 2) = 3 - 3x$

   (d) (i) $1 - (1 - 2x)^2 = 4x - 4x^2$ (ii) $1 - 2(1 - x^2) = 2x^2 - 1$

2 (a) $ct(x) = 9 + 0.4 \times (1.034x) = 9 + 0.4136x$

   (b) The cost in pounds of x cubic feet of gas

3 There are alternative answers for some of the following questions.

   (a) $f(x) = \frac{1}{x}$, $g(x) = 2x + 3$

(b) $f(x) = 2x - 1, \quad g(x) = \sqrt{x}$

(c) $f(x) = \dfrac{1}{x} + 3, \quad g(x) = x^2$

(d) $f(x) = x^4, \quad g(x) = 2x + 1$

(e) $f(x) = x^2 - 4x - 3, \quad g(x) = x^4$

1.2   Range and domain

Give the natural domain and find the corresponding range for the function h such that

$$h(x) = \frac{1}{x^2}$$

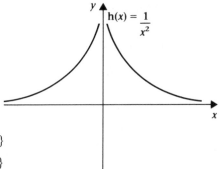

Domain $\{x \in \mathbb{R} : x \neq 0\}$

Range $\{y \in \mathbb{R} : y > 0\}$

Give an example of a function which is one-to-one.

You could choose any function such that each horizontal line cuts the graph of the function at most once.

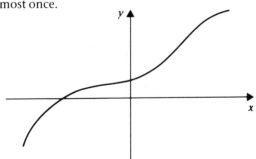

An example is the function f such that

$$f(t) = \tfrac{5}{9}(t - 32), \quad t \geq -459$$

An even simpler one-to-one function is the function whose graph is the line $y = x$.

113

1.3   Inverse functions

(a) Check that f(7) = 20 and f⁻¹ (20) = 7.

(b) Explain the restrictions $x \geq 3$ and $x \geq 4$.

(a) $f(7) = 4^2 + 4 = 20$ $f^{-1}(20) = \sqrt{16} + 3 = 7$

(b) The restriction $x \geq 3$ is applied to f to make the function one-to-one. Then the least value in the range of f is 4, so this is also the least value in the domain of f⁻¹.

1.4   Rearranging formulas

What is the greatest possible domain of the function f⁻¹?

The domain is $x \in \mathbb{R}, x \neq 1$.

E X E R C I S E 2

1   (a) $x = \frac{1}{5}(2y + 3)$ (b) $x = \frac{4}{3}y + 5$

(c) $x = 5 \pm \sqrt{(y - 4)}$ (d) $x = 3 + \dfrac{1}{y}$

2   (a) $f^{-1}(x) = \frac{1}{5}(2x + 3)$; f has domain and range $\{x \in \mathbb{R}\ \}$

(b) $f^{-1}(x) = \frac{4}{3}x + 5$; f has domain and range $\{x \in \mathbb{R}\ \}$

(c) $f^{-1}(x) = 5 + \sqrt{(x - 4)}$; f has domain $x \geq 5$, and range $y \geq 4$

or $f^{-1}(x) = 5 - \sqrt{(x - 4)}$; f has domain $x \leq 5$, and range $y \geq 4$

(d) $f^{-1}(x) = 3 + \dfrac{1}{x}$; f has domain $x \neq 3$, and range $y \neq 0$

3   (a) $a = \dfrac{2y}{900 - y}$

(b) Since a and y are both positive, the denominator $(900 - y)$ must be positive.

4   (a) $(x + 1)y = x - 1$

$\Rightarrow xy + y = x - 1$

$\Rightarrow 1 + y = x - xy = x(1 - y)$

$\Rightarrow x = \dfrac{1 + y}{1 - y}$

(b) In a similar way, $x = \dfrac{2 - 3y}{1 + y}$

5 The image will be $y = f^{-1}(x) = \dfrac{x}{1 - 2x}$

6 $y = \dfrac{1 + x^2}{1 - x^2}$

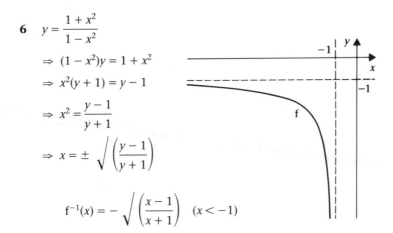

$\Rightarrow (1 - x^2)y = 1 + x^2$

$\Rightarrow x^2(y + 1) = y - 1$

$\Rightarrow x^2 = \dfrac{y - 1}{y + 1}$

$\Rightarrow x = \pm \sqrt{\left(\dfrac{y - 1}{y + 1}\right)}$

$f^{-1}(x) = -\sqrt{\left(\dfrac{x - 1}{x + 1}\right)} \quad (x < -1)$

1.5 Parameters and functions

> (a) What would the formula be for an exchange rate of 9 francs to £1 and a commission of £7?
>
> (b) What would the formula be for an exchange rate of a francs to £1 and a commission of £b?

(a) $f = 9(x - 7)$ (b) $f = a(x - b)$

EXERCISE 3

1 (a) $W = \dfrac{p - b}{a}$ or $\dfrac{1}{a}(p - b)$ (b) $r = \dfrac{C}{2\pi}$

(c) $l = \dfrac{2s}{n} - a$ (d) $r = 1 - \dfrac{a}{s}$ or $\dfrac{s - a}{s}$

(e) $x = \dfrac{yR}{y - R}$ $\left(\text{since } \dfrac{1}{x} = \dfrac{1}{R} - \dfrac{1}{y} = \dfrac{y - R}{yR}\right)$

2 (a) (i) 75 feet   (ii) 175 feet   (iii) 315 feet.

(b) $v = \sqrt{[20(d + 5)]} - 10$ (c) 61.4 m.p.h.

1.6 Functions and transformations of graphs

1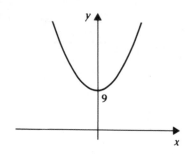

$y = x^2$ translated through $\begin{bmatrix} 0 \\ 9 \end{bmatrix}$

2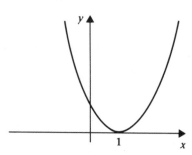

$y = x^2$ translated through $\begin{bmatrix} 1 \\ 0 \end{bmatrix}$

3 $y = \dfrac{3}{x}$ translated through $\begin{bmatrix} -\frac{1}{2} \\ 0 \end{bmatrix}$

4 $y = x^3$ translated through $\begin{bmatrix} 0 \\ -2 \end{bmatrix}$

5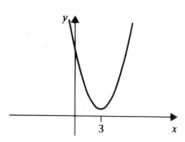

$y = 5x^2$ translated through $\begin{bmatrix} 3 \\ 6 \end{bmatrix}$

6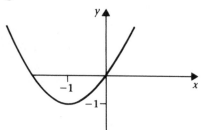

$y = x^2 + 2x = (x + 1)^2 - 1$

i.e. $y = x^2$ translated through $\begin{bmatrix} -1 \\ -1 \end{bmatrix}$

1.7 Combining transformations of graphs

1 (a) $y = (x - 4)^2$ (b) $y = \dfrac{1}{(x - 3)^2}$ (c) $y = -2 - |x|$

(d) $y = 3 - 2(x - 4)^2$ (e) $y = (x + 3)^3 + 2$

(f) $y = (x + 3 - 4)\,\sqrt{(x + 3)} + 1 = (x - 1)\,\sqrt{(x + 3)} + 1$

2 (a) $y = \dfrac{-1}{x+6} - 7$ (b) $y = 3x + 7$ (c) $y = 3 - \dfrac{1}{(x-2)^2}$

2 Circular functions

2.1 Rotation

EXERCISE 1

1 (a) $\sin 50° = 0.77$ (b) e.g. $130°, 410°, 490°, 790°, -230°, -310°$

2 (a) $\cos 163° = -0.96$ (b) $-197°, -163°, 197°, 523°, 557°$

3 (a) $\sin 339° = -0.36$ (b) $201°, 561°, 699°, -21°, -159°$

2.2 Transformations

Which of the graphs A, B, C, D is obtained if

(a) A is reflected in the θ-axis,

(b) B is reflected in the θ-axis,

(c) A is reflected in the y-axis,

(d) B is reflected in the y-axis?

(a) Graph C   (b) graph D   (c) graph C   (d) graph B

Are the effects of these transformations on circular functions consistent with their effects on polynomial functions?

The results **are** consistent with the result previously obtained for polynomial functions.

$y = f(x + p) + q$ is the image of $y = f(x)$ after it has been translated through $\begin{bmatrix} -p \\ q \end{bmatrix}$.

The tasksheet suggests a further result, which can also be shown to be true:
$y = f(bx)$ is the image of $y = f(x)$ under a one-way stretch parallel to the
x-axis with scale factor $\dfrac{1}{b}$.

E X E R C I S E 2

In each case there are alternative correct answers.

1 (a) $y = 2 \cos \theta°$ (b) $y = -3 \sin \theta°$ (c) $y = 10 \cos \theta°$

(d) $y = 4 \cos \theta° + 4$ (e) $y = \sin \theta° + 2$ (f) $y = 3 \sin 2\theta°$

(g) $y = 2 \cos 6\theta° + 1$ (h) $y = 4 \sin (3\theta + 30)° + 3$

2

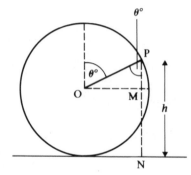

PN = PM + MN

So $h = 0.2 + 0.2 \cos \theta°$

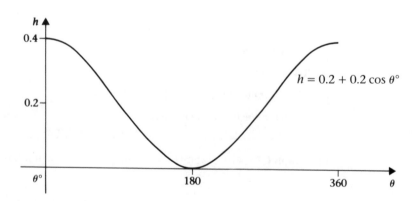

$h = 0.2 + 0.2 \cos \theta°$

2.3 Modelling periodic behaviour

EXERCISE 3

1 (a) (i)   (b)

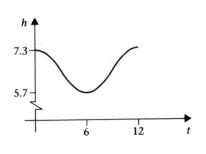

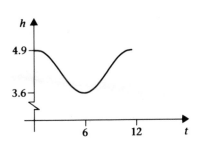

   (ii) $h = 0.8 \cos 30t° + 6.5$ $h = 0.65 \cos 30t° + 4.25$

2 From your first graph you will see that the points from April to October, inclusive, do not conform because of the British Summer Time adjustment. To make the data easier to graph you might proceed as follows:

- subtract 1 hour from sunset times in BST,

- change from hours and minutes to hours written in decimal form,

- count days from 12 December (when sunset is earliest).

  This should give the table shown below, where t is the number of days after 12 December and s is the sunset hour.

t	20	48	76	103	131	159	187
s	16.05	16.75	17.60	18.40	19.18	19.92	20.35

t	215	243	261	299	327	355
s	20.17	19.45	18.43	17.37	16.43	15.90

The graph of s against t is an approximate sine or cosine curve, having amplitude about 2.28 (hours). A possible equation is

$$s = 18.11 - 2.28 \cos\left(\frac{360t°}{365}\right)$$

2.4 Inverse trigonometric functions

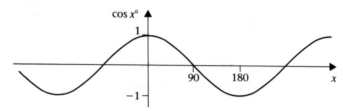

Use your calculator to find the range of principal values of $\cos^{-1} x$.

The range $-90 \leq \cos^{-1} x \leq 90$ is no longer appropriate since cos is an even function.

It is conventional to choose the range $0 \leq \cos^{-1} x \leq 180$ as giving all positive and negative values of $\cos x°$.

EXERCISE 4

1 (a) 11.5° (b) 25.8° (c) −21.1° (d) 137.7° (e) 90° (f) 180°

2 (a) 17.5, 162.5, 377.5, 522.5, −197.5, −342.5

(b) 36.9, 323.1, 396.9, 683.1, −36.9, −323.1

(c) 107.5, 252.5, 467.5, 612.5, −107.5, −252.5

(d) −30, −150, 210, 330, 570, 690

(e) −180, 180, 540

(f) 19.5, 160.5, 379.5, 520.5, −199.5, −340.5

3 (a) (b)

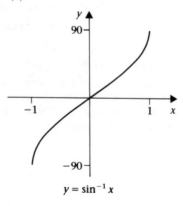

$y = \sin^{-1} x$

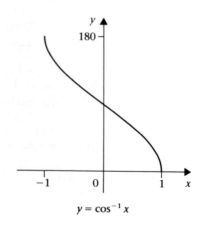

$y = \cos^{-1} x$

2.5   Solving equations

1   (a) $8 \sin 10t° = 5 \Rightarrow \sin 10t° = 0.625$

$\Rightarrow \sin x° = 0.625$ where $x = 10t$

If $0 \le t \le 60$, then $0 \le x \le 600$

$x = 38.7$ or 141.3 or 398.7 or 501.3

$\Rightarrow t = 3.87, 14.13, 39.87$ or 50.13

(b) $7 \cos (t + 35)° = 4$ So, if $x = t + 35$,

$\cos x° = 0.571$

$\Rightarrow x = 55.2$ or 304.8

$\Rightarrow t + 35 = 55.2$ (or 304.8)

$\Rightarrow t = 20.2$, since remaining solutions are not in the required interval.

(c) $\sin (8t - 21)° = -0.75$

$\Rightarrow 8t - 21 = 228.6$ or 311.4 (or 588.6)

$\Rightarrow t = 31.2$ or 41.6

(d) $\cos \frac{1}{2}t° = 0.9$

$\Rightarrow \frac{1}{2}t = 25.8$ (or 334.2)

$\Rightarrow t = 51.6$

2 $5.6 - 4.8 \cos 6t° = 9 \Rightarrow \cos 6t° = \dfrac{-3.4}{4.8}$

$\Rightarrow \qquad t = 22.5, 37.5$

The chair is above 9 metres for $37.5 - 22.5 = 15$ seconds.

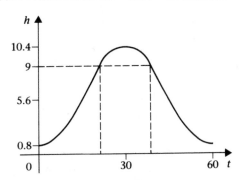

3   (a) $5 + 2.5 \sin 30t° = 6.7 \Rightarrow \sin 30t° = \dfrac{1.7}{2.5}$

$\Rightarrow t = 1.43, 4.57, 13.43, 16.57$

Times: 0126, 0434, 1326, 1634

(b) $5 + 2.5 \sin 30t° = 4.5 \Rightarrow \sin 30t° = \dfrac{-0.5}{2.5}$

$\Rightarrow t = 6.38, 11.62, 18.38, 23.62$

Times: 0623, 1137, 1823, 2337

4 (a) $2 + 1.5 \sin 500t° = 2.75 \Rightarrow \sin 500t° = 0.5$

$\Rightarrow t = 0.06, 0.3$

0.06 and 0.3 second from the start and repeatedly every 0.72 second

(b) $2 + 1.5 \sin 500t° = 2 \Rightarrow \sin 500 t° = 0$

$\Rightarrow t = 0, 0.36, 0.72, \ldots$

Every 0.36 second from the start

(c) $2 + 1.5 \sin 500t° = 3.5 \Rightarrow \sin 500 t° = 1$

$\Rightarrow t = 0.18$

0.18 second from the start and every 0.72 second thereafter

2.6 Tan $\theta°$

E X E R C I S E 6

1 (a) 45°   (b) −80.5°   (c) 0°

2 (a)

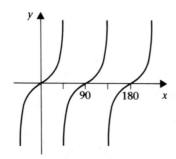

$y = \tan 2x°$

(b)

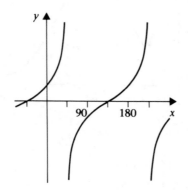

$y = \tan (x + 45)°$

3   (a) $x = 71.6$ or $180 + 71.6 = 251.6$

(b) $\tan (2x + 30)° = 0.8$

   $\Rightarrow 2x + 30 = 38.7$ or 218.7 or 398.7 or 578.7

   $\Rightarrow x = 4.4$ or 94.4 or 184.4 or 274.4

(c) $\tan x° = \pm 1$

   $\tan x° = +1 \Rightarrow x = 45$ or 225

   $\tan x° = -1 \Rightarrow x = 135$ or 315

(d) $4 \sin x° = 3 \cos x°$

   $\Rightarrow \dfrac{4 \sin x°}{\cos x°} = 3$

   $\Rightarrow \tan x° = \dfrac{3}{4}$

   $\Rightarrow x = 36.9$ or 216.9

3 Growth functions

3.1   Exponential growth

> Find the growth factors over successive hundred-year intervals. Is the growth exponential?

Time interval	Growth factor
1650–1750	$\frac{700}{500} = 1.4$
1750–1850	$\frac{1300}{700} = 1.857$
1850–1950	$\frac{2500}{1300} = 1.923$

The growth factors for successive equal time intervals are not constant, so the growth is not exponential.

EXERCISE 1

1

Year	Profit (£ million)	Growth factor
1978	27.0	
1979	32.4	1.2000
1980	38.9	1.2006
1981	46.7	1.2005
1982	56.0	1.1991
1983	67.2	1.2000
1984	80.6	1.1994
1985	96.7	1.1998
1986	116.1	1.2006
1987	139.3	1.1998

Although the growth factors show slight variations, they are all 1.20 to 3 s.f. Allowing for the error introduced in rounding the profit figures, the profit is growing exponentially.

2

Year	Amount (£)	Growth factor (to 3 s.f.)
1985	5450.00	
1986	5940.50	1.09
1987	6475.15	1.09
1988	7057.91	1.09
1989	7693.12	1.09

In each case the annual growth factor is 1.09. This means that the amount in the account at the end of the year is 109% of that at the beginning, so the increase or interest rate is 9%.

Since the growth factor is constant, the growth is exponential.

3

Age	Pocket money (£)	Growth factor
0	50	
1	60	1.2
2	70	1.17
3	80	1.14
4	90	1.13
5	100	1.11

Since the yearly growth factor is not constant, this is not exponential growth.

4 Notice that the time intervals are sometimes 4 years and sometimes 8 years.

Over the 4-year intervals, the growth factor is approximately 1.12 in each case.

Over the 8-year intervals, the growth factor is approximately 1.24 in each case.

Over two 4-year intervals the population would increase by a factor of 1.12 twice, giving an 8-year factor of $1.12 \times 1.12 \approx 1.25$.

The growth is therefore approximately exponential.

5 (a)

Time (s)	0	1	2	3	4	5	6	7	8	9
Charge (v)	9	8	7	6	5	4	3	2	1	0
Growth factor		0.89	0.88	0.86	0.83	0.80	0.75	0.67	0.50	0

The decay is not exponential

(b)

Time (s)	0	1	2	3	4	5
Charge (v)	9	6.75	5.063	3.797	2.848	2.136
Growth factor	0.75	0.75	0.75	0.75	0.75	0.75

The decay is exponential with growth factor 0.75.

3.2 Indices

> Using the context of algal growth, explain what meaning can be given to the expression 2^t when t is 0, -1 and $1\frac{1}{2}$.

In cm^2, 2^0 is the area at the start of the first week.

2^{-1} is what the area would have been a week before.

$2^{1\frac{1}{2}}$ is the area half-way through the second week.

> Are these laws true when a is
>
> (a) negative, (b) 1, (c) 0, (d) a fraction?

(a) When a is negative, the results do not hold, since many values are undefined. For example,

$$(-3)^{\frac{1}{2}} = \sqrt{-3}$$

which cannot be found.

(b) When $a = 1$, the results hold.

(c) Since $0^x = 0$, the results hold for positive values of x. However, 0^0 and 0^{-x} are undefined.

(d) The results hold equally well if a is a fraction.

State which law is used in each stage of the calculation.

The laws used are, respectively

$$a^{-p} = \frac{1}{a^p}, \qquad a^{pq} = (a^p)^q, \qquad a^{1/n} = \sqrt[n]{a}$$

EXERCISE 2

1 (a) 2^5 (b) 2^{10} (c) 2^5 (d) 2^{15}

2 (a) x^5 (b) a^{10} (c) d^5 (d) b^{15}

3 (a) $\frac{1}{9}$ (b) $\frac{1}{1000}$ (c) 27 (d) 125

4 (a) y^{-2} (b) c^5 (c) $x^0 = 1$ (d) x^6

5 (a) 2 (b) $\frac{1}{5}$ (c) $\frac{1}{125}$ (d) 100 (e) 0.1

6 3.32

3.3 Growth factors

Complete the table above and decide if the model is reasonable.

What does the model predict for the population of England and Wales in 1990? Comment on your answer.

t	0	10	20	30	40	50	60
p	15.9	17.9	20.1	22.7	26.0	29.0	32.5
15.9×1.012^t	15.9	17.9	20.2	22.7	25.6	28.9	32.5

Although there is some variation, this model gives results close to the true values.

The model predicts that the population in 1990 would be 15.9×1.012^{149}, that is, 94.0 million. This figure is much higher than the true value of about 49 million. Many factors have affected this, including the world wars, family planning and a different social structure (mothers working outside the home, etc.).

EXERCISE 3

1

Time (hours)	No. of bacteria
0	400
1	2 400
2	14 400
3	86 400
4	518 400
5	3 110 400

(a) There will be 14 400 bacteria after 2 hours.

(b) There will be 1 000 000 bacteria after 4–5 hours.

(c) Since the growth factor is constant, a growth function can be used.

Number of bacteria $= 400 \times 6^t$

2 (a) The growth factor is 1.08.

(b) The value of the investment after n years is £4000 $\times 1.08^n$. When the value is £5000,

$$5000 = 4000 \times 1.08^n$$

Dividing by 4000,

$$1.25 = 1.08^n$$

(c) $n \approx 2.899$. In practice, there would be £5000 at the end of the third year.

3 (a) The growth factor over the 10 days is $\dfrac{2.48}{10} = 0.248$.

The daily growth factor $= (0.248)^{\frac{1}{10}} = 0.87$.

(b) $M = 10 \times 0.87^t$

(c)

t (days)	0	2	3	6	7	10
Mass (kg)	10	7.57	6.57	4.34	3.77	2.48
M	10	7.57	6.59	4.34	3.77	2.48

(d) After 3 weeks, when $t = 21$ the mass is 0.54 kg.

127

(e) Half of the original amount is 5 kg, so

$$5 = 10 \times 0.87^t$$

$$0.5 = 0.87^t$$

$$t = 5$$

Therefore the half-life of bismuth-210 is approximately 5 days.

3.4 Logarithms

(a) Write down the surface area A after t weeks.

(b) How long does it take before the surface area is $5\,m^2$?

(a) Since the initial value is 1, growth factor 2,

$$A = 2^t$$

(b) From the graph, $A = 5$ when $t = 2.3$.

How can you use the table of logarithms shown above to calculate $1.17 \div 1.091$?

From the table,

$$\log_{10} 1.17 = 0.0682$$

$$\log_{10} 1.091 = 0.0378 \text{ (add on the amount given for 1 in the end columns).}$$

Since $\log_{10}\left(\dfrac{a}{b}\right) = \log_{10} a - \log_{10} b,$

$$\log_{10}(1.17 \div 1.091) = \log_{10} 1.17 - \log_{10} 1.091$$

$$= 0.0682 - 0.0378$$

$$= 0.0304$$

Using the table in reverse,

$$\log_{10}(1.073) = 0.0304$$

So

$$1.17 \div 1.091 = 1.073$$

EXERCISE 4

1 (a) $\log_3 9 = 2$ (b) $\log_4\left(\frac{1}{64}\right) = -3$ (c) $\log_{0.5} 4 = -2$

(d) $\log_{\frac{1}{8}} 2 = -\frac{1}{3}$ (e) $\log_{27} 9 = \frac{2}{3}$

2 (a) -2 (b) 3 (c) -1 (d) $-\frac{2}{3}$

3 (a) By the laws of logarithms,

$$\log_3 9 + \log_3 27 - \log_3 81 = \log_3 \left(\frac{9 \times 27}{81} \right) = \log_3 3 = 1$$

(b) $\log_5 15 - \log_5 3 = \log_5 \left(\dfrac{15}{3} \right) = \log_5 5 = 1$

(c) $2 \log_7 \sqrt{7} = \log_7 \sqrt{7} + \log_7 \sqrt{7} = \log_7 (\sqrt{7} \times \sqrt{7}) = \log_7 7 = 1$

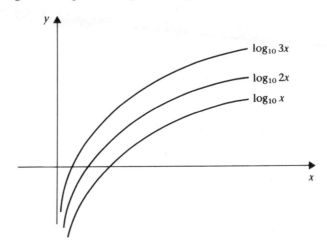

4 The graphs of $\log_{10} 2x$ and $\log_{10} 3x$ can be considered **either** as scalings of $\log_{10} x$ by factors of $\frac{1}{2}, \frac{1}{3}$ from the y-axis **or** as translations in the y direction.

By the laws of logs,

$$\log_{10} 2x = \log_{10} 2 + \log_{10} x = \log_{10} x + 0.3010$$
$$\log_{10} 3x = \log_{10} 3 + \log_{10} x = \log_{10} x + 0.4771$$

5 (a) $\log 1.05 = 0.0212$, $\log 1.267 = 0.1028$

$$\log (1.05 \times 1.267) = 0.0212 + 0.1028 = 0.1240$$
Using the table in reverse, $\log 1.330 = 0.1240$, so
$$1.05 \times 1.267 = 1.330$$

(b) $\log_{10} 10.5 = \log_{10}(10 \times 1.05)$
$$= \log_{10} 10 + \log_{10} 1.05 = 1 + 0.0212 = 1.0212$$
$\log_{10} 1267 = \log_{10}(10^3 \times 1.267) = 3 + 0.1028 = 3.1028$
$\log_{10}(10.5 \times 1267) = 1.0212 + 3.1028 = 4.1240$
Now, since $\log 1.330 = 0.1240$
$4.1240 = 4 + \log 1.330 = \log 10^4 + \log 1.330 = \log 13300$
$10.5 \times 1267 \approx 13300$

6 $\log_5 5! = \log_5 (5 \times 4 \times 3 \times 2 \times 1)$
$= \log_5 5 + \log_5 (4 \times 3 \times 2 \times 1)$
$= \log_5 5 + \log_5 4!$
$= 1 + 1.9746$
$= 2.9746$

129

7   If the colony doubles every hour, it will have grown by a factor of

$$4 = 2 \times 2 \qquad = 2^2 \text{ in 2 hours}$$
$$8 = 2 \times 2 \times 2 \qquad = 2^3 \text{ in 3 hours}$$
$$16 = 2 \times 2 \times 2 \times 2 = 2^4 \text{ in 4 hours}$$
$$2^t \text{ in } t \text{ hours.}$$

The value of t which makes $2^t = 1000$ will be the time it takes to grow by a factor 1000.

$$\log_2 (2^t) = \log_2 1000$$
$$t \log_2 2 = \log_2 1000$$
$$t = \log_2 1000$$
$$2^9 = 512 \text{ and } 2^{10} = 1024$$
$$2^9 < 2^t < 2^{10}$$
$$\Rightarrow\ 9 < t < 10$$

To two decimal places, $t = 9.97$

3.5   The equation $a^x = b$

E X E R C I S E   5

1   (a) $x = 5$ (b) $x = 2.5$ (c) $x = 2.67$

  (d) $x = 2.10$ (e) $x = 1.38$ (f) $x = 2.71$

2   (a) $2 \times 2 \times 2 \times 2 \times 2 = 32 \ \Rightarrow\ 2^5 = 32$

  (b) $9 \times 9 \times 3 = 243 \ \Rightarrow\ 9^2 \times 9^{\frac{1}{2}} = 243 \ \Rightarrow\ 9^{2.5} = 243$

  (c) $8 \times 8 \times 2 \times 2 = 256$
$$\Rightarrow 8^2 \times 2^2 \quad = 256$$
$$\Rightarrow 8^2 \times \left(8^{\frac{1}{3}}\right)^2 \ = 256$$
$$\Rightarrow 8^2 \times 8^{\frac{2}{3}} \quad = 256$$
$$\Rightarrow 8^{2.67} \quad\quad = 256$$

3   (a) The number of bacteria after t hours is given by 250×3.7^t.

  (b) There will be 10000 bacteria when
$$250 \times 3.7^t = 10000$$
$$\Rightarrow \qquad 3.7^t = 40$$
$$\Rightarrow \qquad t = 2.82$$
i.e. after 2 hours 49 minutes

4   The time when there is $\frac{1}{5}$ of the original charge is given by the solution of

$$0.9^t = 0.2$$

i.e. $t = 15.28$ (seconds)

5   The equation used was $1.08^n = 1.25$. $n = 2.90$ (years).

6   The population (in millions) after t years will be 470×1.029^t. When the population reaches one thousand million,

$$1000 = 470 \times 1.029^t$$

$$\Rightarrow 1.029^t = \frac{1000}{470} = 2.128$$

$$\Rightarrow t = \frac{\log 2.128}{\log 1.029} = 26.4$$

i.e. the population will reach one thousand million in 2006.

7   The population of China after t years will be 995×1.014^t. The populations of China and Africa will be equal when:

$$470 \times 1.029^t = 995 \times 1.014^t$$

$$\Rightarrow \frac{1.029^t}{1.014^t} = \frac{995}{470}$$

$$\Rightarrow \left(\frac{1.029}{1.014}\right)^t = 2.117$$

$$\Rightarrow 1.0148^t = 2.117$$

$$\Rightarrow t = 51$$

They will be equal in the year 2031.

4 Radians

4.1   Rates of change

> (a) At what times does the tide rise most rapidly?
>
> (b) At what times does the tide fall most rapidly?
>
> (c) When is the rate of change zero?

(a) The tide rises most rapidly after 0 and 12 hours, at the points where the gradient of the graph is greatest.

(b) The tide falls most rapidly after 6 hours, when the gradient of the graph is most negative.

(c) The rate of change is zero at high and low tides, i.e. after 3, 9 and 15 hours.

(a) Explain why the gradient graph is as shown.

(b) What can you say about the value of k?

(c) Note that the scales on the y- and θ-axes are very different. Roughly how large is k?

(a) Using the ideas of the previous thinking point, you can identify the maxima of the gradient graph at $\theta = 0$ and 360, the minimum at 180 and the zeros at 90 and 270. Between 0 and 90 and between 270 and 360, $\sin \theta °$ is increasing, so the gradient is positive. Between 90 and 270, $\sin \theta °$ is decreasing and so the gradient is negative.

(b) k is the gradient of $y = \sin \theta °$ at the origin.

(c) Very roughly, by joining $(0, 0)$ to $(90, 1)$, $k \approx \frac{1}{90}$

(a) Sketch the gradient graph for $y = \cos x °$.

(b) What do you think is the derivative of:

(i) $\cos x °$, (ii) $\cos x$ (x in radians)?

(a) Sketching the gradient graph of $y = \cos x °$ gives the graph of $\dfrac{dy}{dx} = -k \sin x °$.

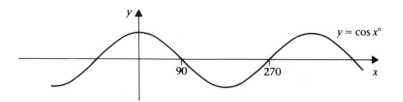

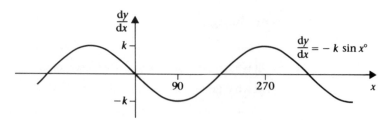

(b) Working in radians, you can make the maximum gradient (i.e. the value of k) equal to 1. So

$$y = \cos x^c \Rightarrow \frac{dy}{dx} = -\sin x^c$$

4.2   Radian measure

EXERCISE 1

1   (a) $\frac{1}{2}\pi$ (b) 2π (c) $\frac{1}{4}\pi$ (d) $\frac{2}{3}\pi$ (e) $\frac{1}{3}\pi$ (f) 4π (g) $-\frac{1}{6}\pi$ (h) $\frac{3}{4}\pi$

2   (a) $45°$ (b) $540°$ (c) $-180°$ (d) $270°$ (e) $-360°$

3 2π

4   (a) 2π (b) 2 (c) $\dfrac{2\pi}{\omega}$

4.3   Area and arc lengths

EXERCISE 2

1   (a) $\frac{1}{2} \times 2^2 \times \frac{1}{4}\pi = \frac{1}{2}\pi$ (b) $2 \times \frac{1}{4}\pi = \frac{1}{2}\pi$ (c) $4 + \frac{1}{2}\pi$

2   The perimeter of CDE $= 2r + r = 3r$
Area CDE $= \frac{1}{2}r^2$
So $3r = \frac{1}{2}r^2$, giving $r = 6$ (since $r = 0$).

3   (a) $800 + (2 \times 400) = 1600\,\text{m}$
(b) Area $= \frac{1}{2} \times 400^2 \times 2 = 160000\,\text{m}^2$
   The largest crowd is 80000.

4   (a) BC $= r \sin\theta$ (b) $\frac{1}{2}r^2 \sin\theta$ (c)$\frac{1}{2}r^2\theta$
(d) Area of segment $=$ area of sector OAB $-$ area of triangle OAB
$$= \tfrac{1}{2}r^2\theta - \tfrac{1}{2}r^2 \sin\theta = \tfrac{1}{2}r^2(\theta - \sin\theta)$$

4.4   More about derivatives

EXERCISE 3

1   (a) $\frac{1}{2}\cos x$ (b) $-5 \sin x$ (c) $0.1 \cos x$
(d) $4 \cos 4x$ (e) $-2\pi \sin 2\pi x$ (f) $0.2 \cos 0.2x$
(g) $-6 \sin 2x$ (h) $3\pi \cos \frac{1}{2}\pi x$ (i) $\cos \frac{1}{3} x$

2   (a) $\dfrac{dy}{dx} = -2 \sin 2x$ (b) $\displaystyle\int \sin 2x \, dx = -\frac{1}{2} \cos 2x$
(c) Since the derivative of $\sin 3x$ is $3 \cos 3x$, $\displaystyle\int \cos 3x \, dx = \frac{1}{3} \sin 3x$.

133

4.5 Applications

Why $\dfrac{5}{12}\pi$?

$$\frac{dh}{dt} = 2.5 \times \frac{\pi}{6}\ \cos\frac{\pi}{6}\,t = \frac{5\pi}{12}\ \cos\frac{\pi}{6}\,t$$

(a) When $t = 4$, what is the value of $\dfrac{dh}{dt}$ to 2 s.f.?

(b) State what this means.

(c) At what other times will $\dfrac{dh}{dt}$ have this value?

(a) $\dfrac{dh}{dt} = \dfrac{5\pi}{12}\cos\dfrac{4\pi}{6} = -0.65 \quad (\mathrm{m\,h^{-1}})$

(b) The tide is falling at a rate of $0.65\,\mathrm{m\,h^{-1}}$.

(c) At 12 hourly intervals, i.e. after $16, 28, 40, \ldots$ hours.

EXERCISE 4

1 (a) $L = 12 + 2.5\cos 2\pi t \ \Rightarrow \ \dfrac{dL}{dt} = -5\pi\sin 2\pi t$

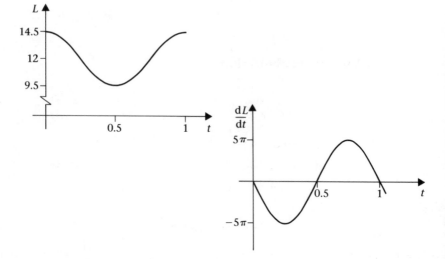

(b)

t	0	0.1	0.25	0.4	0.5
(i) Length (cm)	14.5	14.0	12	10.0	9.5
(ii) Velocity (cm s^{-1})	0	−9.2	−5π	−9.2	0

This represents the motion between the maximum and minimum positions. The velocity is momentarily zero at the extreme positions, and the speed is greatest at the midway position.

2   (a) $h = 0.8 \cos \dfrac{1}{6}\pi t + 6.5 \;\Rightarrow\; \dfrac{dh}{dt} = -\dfrac{2}{15}\pi \sin \dfrac{1}{6}\pi t$

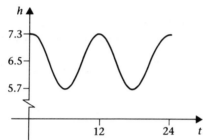

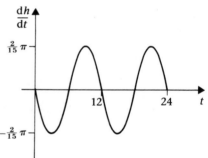

(b) $0.8 \cos \tfrac{1}{6}\pi t + 6.5 = 6 \;\Rightarrow\; \cos \tfrac{1}{6}\pi t = -0.625$

$\Rightarrow\; t = 4.29, 7.71$ (0417 hours and 0743 hours)

When $t = 4.29$, $\dfrac{dh}{dt} = -0.33\,(\text{m h}^{-1})$;   when $t = 7.71$, $\dfrac{dh}{dt} = 0.33\,(\text{m h}^{-1})$.

The rates of change are numerically the same but opposite in sign because in one case the tide is falling and in the other it is rising.

(c)   The tide is falling most rapidly at $t = 3$

$\dfrac{dh}{dt} = -0.42\,(\text{m h}^{-1})$

(d)   Tidal current is greatest when the tide is rising or falling most rapidly and is least near high and low tides.

Depth of water and strength of tidal current are the two important factors in deciding when it is safe to enter or leave harbour.

135

3 (a) $h = 5.6 - 4.8 \cos \frac{1}{30}\pi t \;\Rightarrow\; \dfrac{dh}{dt} = 0.16\,\pi \sin \frac{1}{30}\,\pi t$

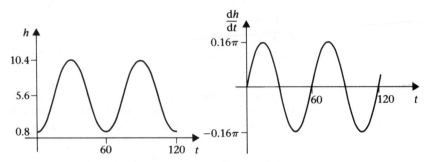

(b) $0.16\pi \sin \frac{1}{30}\pi t = -0.4 \;\Rightarrow\; t = 38.8, 51.2, 98.8, 111.2$
The speed is over $0.4\,\mathrm{m\,s^{-1}}$ between $t = 38.8$ and $t = 51.2$ and again
between $t = 98.8$ and $t = 111.2$. The chair descends most rapidly at
$t = 45$; speed $= 0.5\,\mathrm{m\,s^{-1}}$.

4 (a) (i)

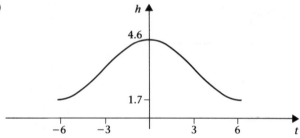

(ii) $h = 3.15 + 1.45 \cos \frac{1}{6}\pi t$

(b) (i)

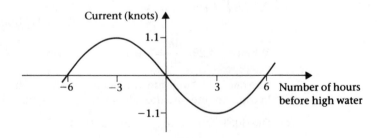

Since the period is 12 hours, $\omega = \frac{2}{12}\pi = \frac{1}{6}\pi$

(ii) $c = -1.1 \sin \frac{1}{6}\pi t$

(iii) Since current represents the rate at which water is entering or
leaving the harbour, this is proportional to the rate of change of
the height of the tide.

(c) (i) $\dfrac{dh}{dt} = -0.76 \sin \tfrac{1}{6}\pi t$

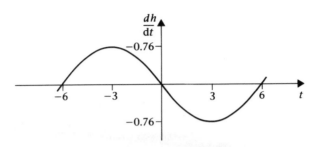

(ii) As indicated above, this is directly proportional to the current, demonstrating the direct relationship between the speed of the current and the rate of rise and fall of the tide.

5 e

5.1 e^x

What is $\displaystyle\int e^x \, dx$?

Recalling that integration is the inverse of differentiation,

$$\int e^x \, dx = e^x \, (+ \text{ constant})$$

EXERCISE 1

1 (a) (i) 20.09 (ii) 164.0 (iii) 0.1353 (iv) 0.249 (v) 1.649

  (b) For many calculators it is 230.2 (to 4 s.f.) because $e^{230.3} > 10^{100}$

2 (a)   (b)

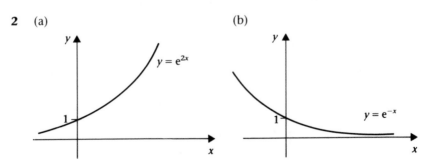

3

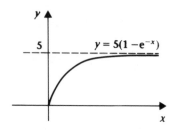

4 (a) (i) When $t = 0$, $y = 5$ (ii) 0.677

(iii)

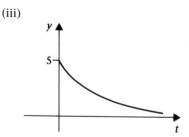

The graph exhibits exponential decay.

(b) Since $0.5 > 0.2$, it decays more rapidly.

5 $y = 4e^t \Rightarrow \dfrac{dy}{dt} = 4e^t = y$

The rate of growth is equal to the size of the colony. It is growing at a rate equal to its size, i.e. at 500 bacteria per hour.

5.2 e^{ax}

> (a) What is $\displaystyle\int e^{ax} \, dx$?
>
> (b) In general, if $\dfrac{d}{dx}(f(x)) = g(x)$, what are
>
> (i) $\dfrac{d}{dx}(f(ax))$ (ii) $\displaystyle\int g(ax) \, dx$?

(a) $\displaystyle\int e^{ax} \, dx = \dfrac{1}{a}e^{ax} + \text{constant}$

(b) (i) $\dfrac{d}{dx}(f(ax)) = a\,g(ax)$

The graph of $f(ax)$ is mapped onto the graph of $f(x)$ by a one way stretch, factor $\dfrac{1}{a}$, from the y-axis. This squashing transformation increases the gradient by a factor of a.

(ii) $\displaystyle\int g\,(ax)\,dx = \dfrac{1}{a}\,f(ax) + \text{constant}$

EXERCISE 2

1 (a) $4e^{4x}$ (b) $-2e^{-2x}$ (c) $\dfrac{d}{dx}(e^x)^5 = \dfrac{d}{dx}(e^{5x})^5 = 5e^{5x}$

(d) $\dfrac{d}{dx}\left(\dfrac{1}{e^{3x}}\right) = \dfrac{d}{dx}(e^{-3x}) = -3e^{-3x}$ (e) $20e^{4x}$ (f) $e^x - \dfrac{1}{e^x}$

(g) $\dfrac{1}{2}e^{\frac{1}{2}x}$ (h) $-45e^{-9x} = -\dfrac{45}{e^{9x}}$

2 (a) $\dfrac{1}{4}e^{4x}$ (b) $-\dfrac{1}{2}e^{-2x}$ (c) $\dfrac{1}{5}e^{5x}$ (d) $-\dfrac{1}{3}e^{-3x}$

(e) $\dfrac{5}{4}e^{4x}$ (f) $e^x - \dfrac{1}{e^x}$ (g) $2\sqrt{e^x}$ (h) $-\dfrac{5}{9e^{9x}}$

The constant of integration has been omitted in all cases.

3 (a)

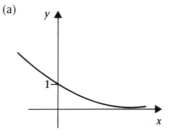

(b)

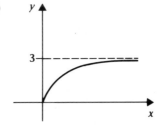

(c)

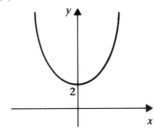

4 (a), (b)

t	0	2	4	6	8
x	10	7.8	6.1	4.7	3.7

(b) 3.7 becomes 13.7 mg.

(c)

t	0	2	4	6	8
x	13.7	10.7	8.3	6.5	5.0

(d)

t	0	2	4	6	8
x	15.0	11.7	9.1	7.1	5.5

t	0	2	4	6	8
x	15.5	12.1	9.4	7.3	5.7

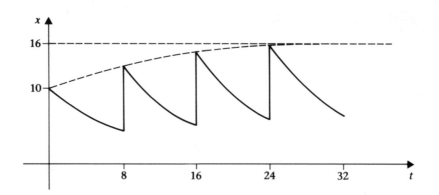

The maximum level of the drug in the body approaches 16 mg, which is approximately 1.6 times the administered dose. (In fact, it can be proved to be $\dfrac{10e}{e-1} = 15.82$ mg.)

5

t	0	2	4	6	8
x	16	12.5	9.7	7.6	5.9 → 15.9

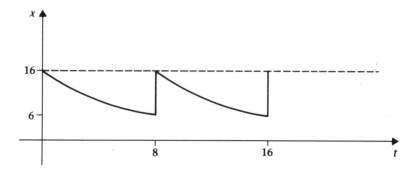

Thus, with a single booster dose, the required level is reached immediately and subsequent doses of 10 mg give a stable level of 16 mg.

5.3   The natural log

> (a) How would you define ln x?
>
> (b) Use your calculator to find   (i) ln $e^{2.3}$ (ii) $e^{\ln 4.3}$
>
>   Explain your results.

(a) By analogy with base 2, ln x is defined so that, if $y = \ln x$, then $x = e^{y}$. ln x and e^{x} are therefore inverse functions.

(b) (i) 2.3   (ii) 4.3

Since ln x and e^{x} are inverse functions, the application of one followed by the other restores the original value.

E X E R C I S E   3

1   (a) 1.25   (b) −1.05   (c) 1.95

2   (a)   (i) ln 3 + ln 4 = ln (3 × 4) = ln 12

   (ii) ln 10 − ln 2 = ln $\frac{10}{2}$ = ln 5

   (iii) 3 ln 5 = ln 5^{3} = ln 125

   (iv) $\dfrac{\ln 20}{\ln 4}$ ≠ ln 5 since this does not correspond to one of the laws of logs.

3   (a) ln x^{3} = 3 ln x (b) ln 4x = ln 4 + ln x

   (c) ln $\frac{1}{3}x$ = ln x − ln 3

141

4 (a) $4 \times \dfrac{1}{x} = \dfrac{4}{x}$ (b) $\dfrac{d}{dx}(\ln x^3) = \dfrac{d}{dx}(3 \ln x) = \dfrac{3}{x}$

(c) $\dfrac{d}{dx}(\ln 4x) = \dfrac{d}{dx}(\ln 4 + \ln x) = \dfrac{1}{x}$

5 90% represents 180 individuals.

$$180 = \dfrac{200}{1 + 199e^{-0.2t}}$$

$\Rightarrow \quad 180(1 + 199e^{-0.2t}) = 200$

$\Rightarrow \qquad\qquad 199e^{-0.2t} = 0.1111$

$\Rightarrow \qquad\qquad e^{-0.2t} = 5.58 \times 10^{-4}$

$\qquad\qquad -0.2t = \ln(5.58 \times 10^{-4})$

$\Rightarrow \qquad\qquad t = -\dfrac{1}{0.2}\ln(5.58 \times 10^{-4}) = 37.5 \text{ (days)}$

6

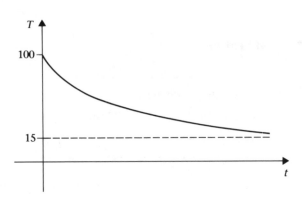

$$40 = 15 + 85e^{-t/8}$$

$\Rightarrow \qquad 25 = 85e^{-t/8}$

$\Rightarrow \qquad e^{-t/8} = \frac{25}{85} = 0.294$

$\Rightarrow \qquad -\dfrac{t}{8} = \ln 0.294$

$\Rightarrow \qquad t = -8\ln 0.294 = 9.8 \text{ (minutes)}.$

7 (a) $\qquad \frac{1}{2}m_0 = m_0 e^{-5570K}$

$\Rightarrow \quad e^{-5570K} = \frac{1}{2}$

$\Rightarrow \quad -5570K = \ln \frac{1}{2}$

$\Rightarrow \qquad K = \frac{-1}{5570}\ln \frac{1}{2} = 1.24 \times 10^{-4}$

(b) $\qquad \frac{9}{10}m_0 = m_0 e^{-1.24 \times 10^{-4}t}$

$\Rightarrow \qquad 0.9 = e^{-1.24 \times 10^{-4}t}$

$\Rightarrow \qquad t = -\dfrac{1}{1.24 \times 10^{-4}}\ln 0.9 = 847 \text{ (years)}.$

6 Transformations

6.1 Graph sketching

In the example above, what would happen if you replaced x with $3x$ **before** you replaced x with $x + 1$?

The equation would become $y = 2e^{3(x+1)}$ instead of $y = 2e^{3x+1}$.

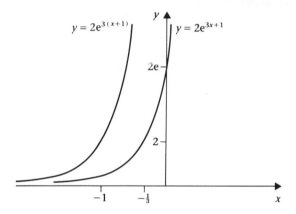

6.2 Stretching a circle

Is y a function of x?

$x^2 + y^2 = 1$ is not the equation of a function. If x is 0.6, for example, then $y = \pm 0.8$. A function can have only one output for any given input.

(a) Describe what effect replacing x with $\frac{1}{3}x$ and y with $(y - 2)$ has on the graph of $x^2 + y^2 = 1$.

(b) Sketch the graph of $(\frac{1}{3}x)^2 + (y - 2)^2 = 1$.

(c) Rearrange the equation into the form $y = \ldots$ so that you can plot the graph.

(a) Replacing x with $\frac{1}{3}x$ and y with $(y - 2)$ gives $(\frac{1}{3}x)^2 + (y - 2)^2 = 1$. The unit circle, $x^2 + y^2 = 1$, is stretched by a factor 3 from the y-axis and then the

resulting ellipse is translated through $\begin{bmatrix} 0 \\ 2 \end{bmatrix}$.

(b)

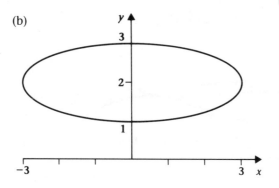

(c) $\frac{1}{9}x^2 + (y-2)^2 = 1 \Rightarrow (y-2)^2 = 1 - \frac{1}{9}x^2 \Rightarrow y = 2 \pm \sqrt{(1 - \frac{1}{9}x^2)}$

EXERCISE 1

1 The equation $y = \ln x$ can be transformed onto $y = \ln 3x$ by replacing x with $3x$. The graph of $y = \ln x$ can therefore be fitted to the graph of $y = \ln 3x$ by a one-way stretch from $x = 0$, factor $\frac{1}{3}$.

The equation $y = \ln 3x$ can be rewritten

$$y = \ln 3x \Rightarrow y = \ln 3 + \ln x \Rightarrow y - \ln 3 = \ln x$$

The equation $y = \ln x$ can be transformed onto $y = \ln 3x$ by replacing y with $y - \ln 3$. The graph of $y = \ln x$ can be fitted to the graph of $y = \ln 3x$ by a

translation $\begin{bmatrix} 0 \\ \ln 3 \end{bmatrix}$.

2 (a) $y = 4x^2 \Rightarrow y = (2x)^2$
The graph of $y = x^2$ can be fitted to the graph of $y = 4x^2$ by a one-way stretch from $x = 0$, factor $\frac{1}{2}$.

(b) $y = 4x^2 \Rightarrow \frac{1}{4}y = x^2$
The graph of $y = x^2$ can be fitted to the graph of $y = 4x^2$ by a one-way stretch from $y = 0$, factor 4.

3 (a) A one-way stretch from $x = 0$, factor 2, followed by a

translation $\begin{bmatrix} 2 \\ 0 \end{bmatrix}$.

Replace x with $\frac{1}{2}x$ then replace x with $x - 2$

$$x^2 + y^2 = 1 \rightarrow (\tfrac{1}{2}x)^2 + y^2 = 1 \rightarrow [\tfrac{1}{2}(x-2)]^2 + y^2 = 1$$

(b) A translation $\begin{bmatrix} 1 \\ 0 \end{bmatrix}$ followed by a one-way stretch from

$x = 0$, factor 2.

Replace x with $x - 1$, then replace x with $\frac{1}{2}x$.

$$x^2 + y^2 = 1 \rightarrow (x-1)^2 + y^2 = 1 \rightarrow (\tfrac{1}{2}x - 1)^2 + y^2 = 1$$

The two equations are equivalent. You are, however, less likely to make a mistake with the translation if you stretch the circle before you translate it.